IN FAR JAPAN

These unique sketches of Japan and Japanese life were written by Frank Hedges, foreign correspondent of the London Times, Christian Science Monitor and the Washington Post. Shrines, mountains, traditional drums, misty rains and the shrill wailing of Shinto music come to life in Hedges' brief, lyrical descriptions, and lovers of Japan are sure to be overwhelmed by memory.

The Kegan Paul Japan Library

Editorial Advisors
Peter Hopkins and Kaori O'Connor

The National Faith of Japan •	*D.C. Holtom*
The Japanese Enthronement Ceremonies •	*D.C. Holtom*
History of Japanese Religion •	*Masaharu Anesaki*
Ainu Creed and Cult •	*Neil Gordon Munro*
Japan: Its Architecture, Art and Art Manufactures •	*Christopher Dresser*
An Artist's Letters from Japan •	*John La Farge*
Japanese Girls and Women •	*Alice M. Bacon*
The Kwaidan of the Lady of Tamiya •	*James S. de Benneville*
The Haunted House •	*James S. de Benneville*
We Japanese •	*Frederic de Garis and Atsuharu Sakai*
Shogi: Japanese Chess •	*Cho-Yo*
The Nightless City of the Geisha •	*J. E. de Becker*
Landscape Gardening in Japan •	*Josiah Conder*
Things Japanese •	*Basil Hall Chamberlain*
The Gardens of Japan •	*Jiro Haneda*
Ancient Japanese Rituals and the Revival of Pure Shinto •	*Sir Ernest Satow with Karl Florenz*
History of Japanese Thought •	*Hajime Nakamura*
The Mikado's Empire •	*W. E. Griffis*
Quaint Customs and Manners of Japan •	*Mock Joya*
Japanese Homes and Their Surroundings •	*Edward S. Morse*
Japanese Buddhism •	*Charles Eliot*
Lafcadio Hearn's Gleanings in the Buddha-Fields •	*Lafcadio Hearn*
In Far Japan •	*Frank H. Hedges*
Japanese Aspects and Destinies •	*W. Petrie Watson*
Lafcadio Hearn's Japan •	*Lafcadio Hearn*
A History of Japan •	*Hisho Saito*
Japan As It Was And Is •	*Richard Hildreth*
The Japanese Nation •	*Inazo Nitobe*

YOSHINO SHRINE

The Shrine of the Emperor Godaigo
—who sacrificed himself for his
people and his country

IN FAR JAPAN

GLIMPSES AND SKETCHES

FRANK H. HEDGES

LONDON AND NEW YORK

First published in 2005 by
Kegan Paul Limited

Published 2016 by Routledge
2 Park Square, Milton Park, Abingdon, Oxfordshire OX14 4RN
711 Third Avenue, New York, NY 10017

First issued in paperback 2016

Routledge is an imprint of the Taylor and Francis Group, an informa business

© Taylor and Francis, 2005

Distributed by:
Marston Book Services Ltd
160 Milton Park
Abingdon
Oxforshire OX14 4SD
United Kingdom

All Rights reserved. No part of this book may be reprinted or reproduced or utilised in any form or by any electric, mechanical or other means, now known or hereafter invented, including photocopying or recording, or in any information storage or retrieval system, without permission in writing from the publishers.

ISBN 13: 978-1-138-97241-4 (pbk)
ISBN 13: 978-0-7103-1076-7 (hbk)

British Library Cataloguing in Publication Data

Library of Congress Cataloging-in-Publication Data
Applied for.

This book is laid in offering, as
should be all first fruits
before my Mother

A WORD OF WARNING AND ACKNOWLEDGMENT

There are as many facets to life in Japan as in America, in England, or elsewhere. Here and there a book may be written that catches the reflected light from more than one such. A few books have attempted to revolve about the whole life of this people and this nation of Japan, to give a photograph of the unit: I believe the result is usually the bedazzled confusion of the beholder. All I ask is that those who read the pages to follow remember that they do not picture Japan in its entirety, but give only the reaction created by a glimpse of life, past and present, in Japan. They will be more enjoyed, pleasured, even understood I believe, if read piecemeal and at many short sittings instead of continuously.

They are fragmentary; so are the impressions that come to us in life. We do not in one swift moment gain full and complete insight, but bit by bit weave together disconnected strands that make the imperfect whole on which we base our poor judgments. Here are offered merely a few such strands. No judgment should be based on them, for they afford only a tiny part of the knowledge needed for sound conclusions. Accept these fragments, gain others, many others, from other sources, and then perhaps, if you still wish, catalogue and classify this people and this nation of the Fartherest East.

The courtesy of more than one American and British periodical has made possible the reproduction of certain of these sketches originally published by them in part or in whole. This courtesy is appreciated.

The debt to friends in Japan and of Japan who have helped me to see with their eyes, with their hearts, and with their wisdom, is acknowledged; it can not be discharged.

F. H. H.

FOREWORD

It is the fleeting breath of a vanishing civilization that I would grasp and crystallize in these brief sketches, that in their turn must fade and perish.

The Japan of the Past, with all its imperfections, with all its loveliness, is vanishing from the face of the earth, is already dimming in the memories of man.

It was an alluring civilization that was builded by Japan. If not based on aestheticism, still it was colored, made beautiful, entrancing by an artistry of the commonplace that is more pervasive in its charm than all the poppies that bring poppy dreams. The Japan of other days was a world of cruelty, of savagery, perhaps, in its stark nakedness of man's thirst for power. Thrown about its brutal truths of life floated a gossamer veil of sheer loveliness. At times the folds that catch the eye conquer by their severe simplicity; again, it may be an artistic symbolism, or a childlike, trustful joy, or some other phase peculiar unto itself.

This gossamer veil is shrivelling, has almost shrivelled, in the broad glare of the sun that streams from out the West. It can not be otherwise. If choice there ever were, the time for choosing has long passed. The Japan of today is not, the Japan of tomorrow cannot be, that Japan of the retreating Past.

There linger still, here and there, for him who

has the eyes to see, the ears to hear and the heart to echo back, the glimpses of this past heritage and charm. Old Japan may linger in some wayside, tree-embowered shrine or in the way a wave breaks on the coast. The voiceless ghost of some long-dead hero may stir it into life for a fleeting moment. It may speak for a brief second in the heart-memory of some youth or maid caught in the toils of Japan's readjustment to a prosaic world. It is such treasured gleams as these that I have sought to imprison in weak words.

Politics and economics, world relations, all those standards used most often by the Western world to judge Japan must needs be laid aside. There are places for them, and none is more ready to deal with them in those places than I.

Here, all that has been attempted is to put into English the charm of Old Japan that can still be felt by the diligent, even half-attuned searcher.

CONTENTS

	Page
Dedication	v
A Word of Warning and Acknowledgment	vii
Foreword	ix
See Revealed!	1
A Thousand Steps of Stone	2
Drums of the Mountains	5
When Rains Descend	9
Color	11
The Bridge	13
The Foreigner Arrives	17
Young Japan	25
The Spring Equinox	26
Nyubai, or the Rainy Season	27
Sunshine and Summer	28
Flower of the Buddha	32
"The Pines Are in Their Glory"	33
The Mountain Top	37
One in Each Generation	40
The Mountain Spat It Forth	44
The Politician	46

A Gift for a Gift	49
The Hakone in Winter	51
"Blows the Cherry"	53
At Noon	58
An Overcrowded Empire	60
The Priest Is Dead	64
Toshogu	66
When the Dead Return	71
The Spider	76
A Saint at Peace	78
Coast and Cliff	82
The Desire for Friends	86
The Modern Mecca	88
The Children	90
"Merry Kurisumasu"	93
A Japanese Home	96
When One Is Host	101
Flux	103
A Stranger	104
Faith	105
The Plums Are Blossoming	106
Ichi Riki	110
The Seventh Night of the Seventh Month	112
This Morning	115
May Day	117

The Immigration Law	119
Service Completed	123
Japan in Manchuria	126
Forebodings	128
The Internationale	131
Azalea	133
Rooftrees	134
Snow	135
The Heralds of Spring	136
A Japanese Cape Cod	140
The Kimigayo	145
The City	148
Throughout the Day	149
What We Call Progress	153
Gardens	159
Ghosts of Kamakura	161
The Most Sacred Rite	165
The Seal of Japan	176
The Emperor	180
Along the Coast	192
The Ueno Mausolea	194
"Like a Mighty Army"	196
From the Eighth Century	198
The Moon of Asia	207
Lost Rapture	208

"Wassho! Wassho! Wassho!"	212
An Old-Fashioned Garden	216
Shinmiri	221
The Fragrance of Friendship	223
Chame San	224
Gift of Poems	229
Non-Completeness	232
The Earthquake-Dead	233
True Tribute	239
Asakusa Park	241
Sunset and Moonrise	243
The Outcast	245
Happiness in the Hakone	248
When It Is Cold	253
The Snow Comes	255
At Matsushima	258
The Ginza	263
From Peking to Tokyo	269
Bearers of Wood	274
Far From Echigo	275
The Mendicant	280
The Inn	281
Afoot in Izu	282
Looking at Japan	288
Victory!	289

The Poems of Japan	291
The Moon of March	296
The World Awakens	299
A Happy Land	301
A First Principle	309
Pioneers of Empire	310
Japan's Gift	313
Nihon no Koe	317
My Lord of Sendai	321
The Western Weavers	325

See Revealed!

DRAW back the shoji!

Through the opened casement in the stream of golden sunlight glimmers the pure white wonder of O Yama, the green, green pine-clad hills and fertile rice plains of the Eight Great Islands, the clouds of pale pink cherry bloom and the heart of a race, to whom the beautiful is as daily bread, of a race proud of its ancestry and its inheritance, delicately sensitive to the barbed criticism of the Western World and eager to win to the gift of comradeship with all the peoples of the earth.

A Thousand Steps of Stone

FROM where the blue waves of Sagami Bay break on the rocks to die in foaming glory, a thousand steps of stone lead upward to the mountain far above and to its ancient shrine to a most ancient god. Up through the little village known as Idzusan they mount, straight and unswerving as the flight of an arrow. The soft luxury of the coast with its inns and hot springs is disdained in this ascent of rough hewn stones. There is no deviation to the left or right, for the Way of the Gods knows naught of compromise.

The beach is left below and the town drops steadily away as step after step, brief terrace after terrace, is ascended. Slowly the great width of the bay unfolds itself. On one hand the cliffs of the Miura Peninsula, Enoshima, Kamakura are glimpsed through the golden haze that hovers over the Pacific; on the other the high wooded peaks of Idzu stretch into the water, a serrated row of beauty, the crenelations of the ancient castle of a rude giant who sleeps and wakes, and sleeps again beneath Japan. The green slopes of Hatsushima that lie wrapped in daffodils rise from the waters of the bay, and beyond in the far distance, towers the crest of Oshima with its pillar of white smoke ascending like a cloud of incense from an earthly censor, seeking to propitiate the wrath that all too frequently shakes these islands of Japan with terror and destruction.

One by one the steps ascend the mountainside, climbing to the heights above at an angle almost perpendicular. A torii arches over the ascent, and higher still a cut bamboo reaches from branch to branch of sentinel trees across the path of stone, a cut bamboo from which depends a thick rope of rice straw like to that which binds the rock of heaven so that nevermore may the Heavenly Shining Deity hide her face from the world of men.

On up and up, and the handiwork of human beings dwarfs in the scene below. Steel rails gleam where the new railway creeps from out one tunnel to enter another, the railway that is the easy path of modern civilization, the "Way of the Century," a strange contrast to these thousand steps of stone that so long have been the Way of the Gods to the children of Japan.

One by one, slowly and with labored breath, the steps are climbed. As the mountain top is neared terraced rice fields yield their place to pine and cryptomeria in this too early spring, to bamboo, cherry, plum; the fields are gone and the forest is entered.

Green moss and white-gray lichens form a patina that overlays the simple torii, the stone lanterns, steps and encircling wall of the shrine grounds. A pine that seems, but only seems, to be as old as the mountain itself spreads dark branches of green needles over one corner of the terrace, its huge trunk rising from the damp, bare soil that never feels the sun. Two tiny, tiny pines, one on each side of the open shrine, have just been planted, and around them hangs the spirit-rope of rice straw with its fluttering paper offerings. Even the giant tree must go some day, and these two striplings of the forest are to inherit its guardianship of this mountain shrine. The old tree stirs in murmuring accents of protection. The soft, restless voice of the forest is to be heard now instead of the roaring boom of surf so far below.

The shrine itself is old. Its carved, weather-beaten entranceway tells the tale of passing winters, of rain and snow and sunshine, of storm and of fair weather. Three Imperial chrysanthemums of gold gleam from the rooftree, truly emblematic of the sun itself which gives their shining petals life against the dark background of pine needles.

Although Spring has not as yet caressed the Kwanto into a rebirth of beauty, the white blossoms of a mountain cherry form a cloud of fleecy purity in one corner, while the dying petals of a plum flutter to the ground beneath the grove of pines and of bamboo.

The giant trees whisper of the past, the present and the future, of unchanging and eternal truth. Through their branches, out across the terrace on the heights, is seen the sun-kissed ocean; the ancient shrine stands silently behind.

From far below comes softly, faintly, the chant of workmen moving rocks and stones and tunneling the mountain for man's comfort, but their world seems as distant and remote as the dim murmur of their song. The tree-shrouded shrine that marks the end of the thousand steps of stone lies enwrapped in the spirit of the days of Jimmu Tenno, in the solemn serenity of primaeval grandeur, when all life was simple and man fought and loved and died and bowed in simple faith before his gods.

Drums of the Mountains

THE mists, that are more characteristic of gray and green Japan than is the autumn sunshine which kisses the chrysanthemums into life, swirled about the narrow valley high in the mountains and caught in the tops of the tall pine trees.

In a great marquee of red and white striped bunting a celebration was being held, a celebration at which speeches were being made by men clothed in the coat and trousers of the West. All of the utiliarian ugliness of the strange mixture of present-day Japan was being aired under the wind-swayed canopy that protected these men and their ill-fitting garments from the soft caress of mountain mists.

From above and far below reverberated the sound of drums, for the dwellers in the mountains, the simple country folk of the district, were celebrating in their own way, in the way of Old Japan. In the streets of the village and scattered all along the mountain road they were making merry. Not for them the "high collars" that were uncomfortable. It was a gala day and they were garbed in their festival kimono.

Singers were going about from place to place, retelling the old, old stories in the peculiar falsetto so admired by their countrymen. Lion dances were being held, dances almost as old as the mountains themselves and yet ever new to those who dance and to those who watch. And everywhere the boom of drums reverberated, insistent, all-pervading, more tangible than the swirling mists which caught and broke into trailing shreds with each gentle puff of wind or which touched the cheek with soft dampness as if seeking the warmth of more virile life.

Incessant, steady, deep-toned and seeming to fill the whole of the mountains came the boom, boom of the drums of Japan. It sounded and resounded from the mountain sides and echoed through the narrow valley. It rose from the gorge below, drowning the voice of the torrent which rushed among gray rocks. It floated down more gently but nonetheless solidly from the heights up which the road wound as it left the village. Drums, drums, drums—the strange rhythm of a strange race.

That night the lanterns along the side of the road were lit and the festival carts of other days were drawn along. To this one was harnessed a great bullock which strained and tugged to right and left. Another was pushed along by men hidden deep within its interior. But most of them were drawn by many, many children, a hundred, perhaps, to the cart, who struggled with one another for the honor and whose childish treble as they panted in time to their motions formed a curious overtone to the deep resonance of the never-ceasing boom of drums.

Through the twisting street of the little mountain hamlet the heavy carts creaked and groaned as they moved slowly, threatening now and again to topple against the glass front of some shop more prosperous and pretentious than its neighbors and so able, like the men of the morning in the red and white marquee, to dress itself in the fashion of the Western World. There was almost the hope that this would happen, that the cart and the deities enshrined therein would pronounce judgment against the sacrilegious desecration of the picturesque, as the mikoshi in other days had rendered crude but withal effective communal justice when judges and juries were not even names in the mountains and on the plains of the Eight Great Islands, the Land of Fertile Rice Ears.

Surely the gods of the past could do no better service than to crush out some of the hideous architectural monstrosities with which their worshippers have saddened the nation.

The mist was torn asunder for a fleeting breath by a gust of wind, and forth into the circlet of moonlight and of starlight stepped the girl dancers, three little maids wreathed in smiles at this, their triumphal moment. They, too, were of the village, with their faces painted for the festival, wearing kimono more lovely than their everyday attire and with broad obi so knotted as to show their tender years.

One was but six, and one thirteen, while the third formed a gradation between these two as they clapped their hands in unison to booming of the drums and the shriller screeching of a flute of reeds that now took up the even-timed monotone of ceaseless sound.

The dance was none too graceful and the three young dancers none too perfect in their art, but who among that crowd of mountain villagers was there to criticize the technique of sheer joy and happiness?

Bending and swaying with the boom and the screech of the music and with the twanging whine of the samisen of some strolling player, they danced there in the brief second of moonlight and on into the duller yellow glow shed by myriad lanterns of rice paper as the mists again closed in over the mountain to reclaim their own. It was a posture dance that their mothers and grandmothers had danced before them, that the villagers had seen each year throughout their lives and that the mountains had seen for many centuries as the season of the matsuri rolled around again and again. It was an old, old dance of an ancient people, and yet the freshness of youth and of laughter was born of it.

And the drums boomed on. They echoed through the night and re-echoed until it seemed that one was living, moving in their steady rhythm, that it, like the mists, had closed down all about and was a part of the very atmosphere, of life itself.
On into the night, relentless, unceasing, eternal it seemed, came the measured boom, boom, boom of the drums of Japan, the drums of the mountains, the drums of joy, the drums of the past and the present and the drums that would go on with their changeless rhythmic boom, boom, boom into the unknown future that is yet to come.

When Rains Descend

MISTS curling about the sharp-edged mountains that tower from the sea and gently falling rain from a gray sky seem more characteristic of Japan than does sunshine. Statistics tell the tale of how, in normal years, one city averages two hundred twenty-six wet days and the driest of all has one hundred forty-five days of rain. They who knew Tokyo or Kyoto or other spots before sidewalks came and when the streets were often veritable seas of mud were provoked into believing that the Japanese should adopt as their national emblem the umbrella and the high wooden geta that raise them above the slushy puddles of the thoroughfare.

The nyubai, the rainy season that comes with the heat of June, quickens the life of plants, whose growth from day to day can almost be perceived, but it wilts men. The beauty of the cherry blossom season is a breathless beauty that is grasped hurriedly, for there is always present the consciousness that with the coming of the night a storm may rise with rain and wind that will sweep the delicate pink petals from the branches of the trees. No plans can be made except with a proviso for alteration in case of rain.

And yet, despite the mud and discomforts of being wet, rain is a thing of beauty in Japan. The wood block prints most prized by Japanese themselves are those in which rain slants across the face of the picture or falling snow partially obscures the outlines of buildings and human beings. On a rainy morning every jinrikisha is pressed into use. The little carriages are tightly closed to protect their occupants, but the 'rikisha puller is exposed to the elements.

There are few more artistic sights to be found than the 'rikisha man of Japan, if he be young and strong. He runs gently through the rain without apparent effort, the 'rikisha bumping along behind him. His well-muscled brown legs are bare except where splashed with mud. Cloth shoes with rubber soles and a pocket for the great toe are on his feet. White trunks like those of the college track man in the West are topped by a tight-fitting sateen jacket of black, or by a square-cut coat of dark blue stuff, the emblem of this firm stamped or embroidered on his back. A stiff cap or a wide mushroom hat completes the scanty costume.

Farmers, leading their horses through the streets to the marketplace, are garbed in rice straw that makes each seem a living haystack.

Dainty Japanese maidens prick their way through the mud, their outer kimono of dark materials raised to reveal underskirts of scarlet, saffron or bright blue. Everywhere are the oiled paper umbrellas of Japan, their subdued colors softened even more by the gray rain.

Color

GORGEOUS beyond description are the dry goods shops of Japan. Deep purples and brilliant, joyful reds; greens as softly delicate as leaves but half unfurled or as fiercely challenging as the freshly cut rind of a watermellon; the golden glitter of metal threaded embroideries; saffron and burnt amber and sky blue and turquoise; a dash of midnight darkness and pure, snowy whiteness; the open shop front gashes with its riot of color the long gray line of monotonous unpainted wood that makes the street in Japan.

With children on their backs young wives pause to gaze at the beauty of cotton and silk, the figured patterns and the gay designs of broad-banded obi. Garbed in more sombre clothing, the elder women finger bolts of goods, selecting and rejecting for their daughters and their daughters-in-law. Each piece is just enough for one kimono or an obi. This is a pattern for a child of three, that for a woman of forty.

In the cities there are larger stores, housed in great buildings of brick and stone, with elevators, cash girls, counters and all the contrivances of the West, but it is the little shop of Old Japan whose lure is irresistible. With each sunrise the dull boards that close the shop at night are removed, to be replaced by multi-colored banners of the goods for sale. The sunlight strikes across them, and with the falling shadows their gay shades dance happily in the flickering glow of paper lanterns.

The Bridge

A WIDE wooden bridge arches over one of the tidewater canals that wend their way through the whole of the lower part of Tokyo. It is like unto an hundred of its fellow-bridges, rising gently from each end, its floor boards covered with a thick layer of soil and gravel, its squared posts unpainted and worn by the weather to that drab grayness which is the characteristic tone of neutral-tinted Tokyo.

At one time it gave entrance to the outer grounds of the Shogun's palace, to that wide enclosure which afforded space for the mansion-homes of feudal retainers who thus formed a living barricade about the inner precincts of the castle. Therefore, it has a noble name, a double name, remembrance of the days when it was both a bridge and gate.

Those days are gone. The over-crowded trams of a congested city in a densely populated Empire now clang and bump along the bankway of the brackish canal. Not even the ghosts of the brilliantly clad samurai, each with his two swords and part-shaven pate surmounted by a topknot, can be conjured up when the sun beats down or when the rains of Japan wrap all in their gray mistiness. No cherry blossoms touch the scene to glory in the month of April, and when October comes not a single scarlet maple leaf drifts down to rest a moment on the bridge in flaming beauty before crushed underfoot by coolie, cart or motor car.

This is the bridge, its atmosphere, its color and its lack of personality on most the days and during most the hours.

It is not always thus. There are moments, minutes, now and again a longer space of time, when a film of enchantment is thrown about and envelops this prosaic bit of everyday life.

Such was the early September morning, that bright, hot September morning, which was the first that ever I spent in Japan. Where was the color, enchantment, gaiety that form the average Westerner's misconception of Japan? Not at the dock at Yokohama, surely. Strangeness and incongruities, some of them ludicrous, were there, but naught of beauty. Not in the ride by electric train to Tokyo, through alleys, stone-banked cuts or looking out over dark housetops to factory chimneys. Not in the first impression gained of the capital city of Japan, nor yet in the first crossing of the bridge.

But the coming back over its earth-covered boards was different. A young workman, garbed in a square-cut coolie coat of darkest blue with the symmetrical ideographs of his firm stamped on the back in white, bare from his mid-thighs downward to his white-shod feet and with his well-muscled, brown-skinned legs moving in healthy rhythm, was swinging across the bridge, brimming with the joy of life. He saw the foreigner, eyes filled with wonderment no doubt, a stranger in the land. He stared a moment in return as is the wont of him and all his countrymen, and then his face became a smile as he ducked his close-cropped head in a little bow that seemed to be a welcome to Japan.

Again, when twilight falls and the last glow of effluescent sky is mirrored for a moment by the inky surface of the ill-smelling moat-canal, there comes a brief gleam of beauty midst the drabness, of beauty that is like a breath of mountain air to the parched lungs of a dweller on the plains in mid-summer.

A broad band of liquid rose stretches westward underneath the bridge. Irregular buildings, so ugly in the sunshine, rise in the semi-shadows like the crenellated wall of an ancient battlement. It has been worth living through the day for this.

A few seconds, minutes, half an hour at most, and darkness comes to be pricked into sensient being by the twinkling lights of modern buildings that stretch eastward from the bridge, following the angles and the curves of this ancient, man-made strip of stone-embanked sea water whose first duty was protection. Tonight it serves as a dark mirror to reflect and double in its depths man's conquest of the night.

Some times by noon, some times in mid-morning, and again when the sun has begun its swift descent toward the horizon a scene unfolds that ends the drabness of the everyday. Barges, low in the water from their heavy loads, have spread square sails in the heart of the city to catch what breeze there be. The tide is in, and the dirty water stretches deep and wide as the boats move slowly along. The sails and masts will have to be lowered to pass beneath the bridge, and bargees will bend their utmost strength at the end of long poles, but what matter? That will be in a minute. Just now the sails are like a flight of wild geese in their winged passage north or south in obedience to instinct.

The bridge is like a faded print of Hiroshige, Hokusai. Gray and dull, the picture that it makes is one of clear-cut line, a naturalistic etching that is accepted as a part of life and stirs not the emotions. But here and there, despite the ageing of the print, a trace of color lingers. There is the smile of welcome, the sunset glow, the pricking lights of fairyland, the flight of geese against the blue of Heaven far, far above drab gayness, dirty water, above all the momentarily inconsequential things of life.

The Foreigner Arrives

DISAPPOINTMENT wells over the average foreigner as the liner on which he has crossed the Pacific ties up at the dock at Yokohama. The excitement that comes with landing on foreign soil does not conquer this disappointment as he steps into a jinrikisha and is trotted through the modern streets of the port city to the railway station. If he catch the electric train to Tokyo, he is further depressed during this ride of forty, fifty minutes, and the drab and non-exotic appearance of the capital city certainly does not serve to cheer him up.

He does not see the Japan which he has visioned. Instead of a riot of brilliant colors, the whole land has taken on a universal gray. Dinky little trolley cars that bounce through the streets over uneven rails carry more passengers than fall to the lot of the fast-disappearing, sturdy, bare-limbed 'rikisha runner. Unless he be so fortunate as to land during a brief ten-day period in April, not only are the cherry blossoms absent but he catches only one or two quick glimpses of flowers of any description. In all likelihood, falling rain or drifting mists have blotted out the glory of Fuji-san where the sacred mountain towers over the harbor, for rain, rather than sunshine, is the normal condition of Japan.

He has probably read a bit of Lafcadio Hearn and

has fallen under the lotus spell of that master of descriptive English and lover of the soul of Japan. Or perhaps his friends have recommended the book written by some tourist who spent the whole of a solid month gathering his material. Certain it is that whether he has read a word or not about the Sunrise Isles he has absorbed the belief that they lie wrapped in sunshine, girdled with flowers and filled with a happy, laughing people. None of this does he see on his first day in Japan—if he be honest with himself.

The cities of Japan are far from beautiful; the countryside is another matter. It is the cities which the newly arrived foreigner sees first. Because he admires the graining of wood more than the colors of paint, the Japanese refuses to bury timber under a banket of white or yellow or green, red, blue, brown or whatnot. Here and there stands a building that has been coated with plaster or stucco or that is made of brick, but most of the streets are lined with rows of small weather-beaten houses. The newness of wood soon turns to a uniform gray as the rains beat down upon it. The roofs are of black or gray tiles or of corrugated iron. The wonderful gardens lie hidden behind tall fences and walls. Even the surface of the streets takes on this gray tone, whether they be paved or of muddy gravel and without sidewalks.

Japan has been peculiarly unfortunate in her choice of foreign architecture. Of the older, the pre-earthquake buildings there is scarcely one which is not an affront to the eye. Not only are they out of keeping with Japan, but they would be passed by with a shudder in any city of the Western World.

This was due, it is to be supposed, to lack of experience, lack of background, and therefore lack of discrimination. Seventy years ago the whole of Western civilization was an unread book to the Japanese, a book that fascinated and captivated them. In their eager desire to absorb its contents they did not pass over the bad and take only the good, but adopted the whole bodily. The architectural monstrosities of the earlier foreign-style buildings of Tokyo and other cities of Japan are but one manifestation of this. Fortunately, there has come a reaction, and Japan today is erecting some few buildings that would grace any capital with their beauty.

When Frank Lloyd Wright created the new Imperial Hotel he expressed the hope that it would serve as a foundation for a whole new school of architecture for Japan. There has been great criticism of the hotel; and equally great praise. As an investment and from a purely utilitarian point of view, much of this adverse criticism has been justified; structurally, the building proved its worth in the numerous earthquakes which it has successfully ridden, while from the artistic standpoint few, if any, buildings of the present world generation can compare with it.

It was probably because the hotel defied the earthquake waves so well that thousands of the citizens of Tokyo have come to regard it as the model for new buildings to replace those which were destroyed. Mr. Wright has succeeded in creating a new school of architecture in Tokyo, but if he were to return to Japan today he would be heartsick. The hotel is a perfect artistic unit; scarcely a one of the new buildings which have borrowed from it have caught its spirit. Where the design has been reproduced in piece-meal or in fragmentary manner throughout the capital, the result has all too often been but freakish.

Lines and angles that were worked out to perfection in the lava, the dull yellow brick and the pierced copper with its patina of green are apt to be bizarre and grotesque in wood and plaster. The harmonious proportions of the great building have not often been adhered to in its reproductions. The copyists have been but copyists and they have not been ever accurate in that sphere. They have copied some one or two or half a dozen details; nowhere have they copied the magnificent unity of the whole structure.

Scarce a block of structures in post-earthquake Tokyo that does not display one or more notes borrowed from the hotel. They are immediately recognizable, for the architecture is unique and individual. Colors that only a master would dare to combine are harmoniously blended in the hotel; in its imitations they are frequently grotesque or pitifully tragic. Projecting ledges of lava and hanging terraces in the original building become almost laughable when rendered into square wooden blocks of unpainted timber or stucco. Oddly shaped ornaments that go to make up the artistic unit of the hotel look like the unwelcomed dreams of a futurist when placed next four square panes of glass.

The newer type of Western building, modelled on American skyscraper architecture, is either actively plain and cheerless or has a fancifully decorated front, all attempts at beauty having been concentrated on the face of the building as if it were but a bit of cardboard or decoration for the stage. Among them are a few that are artistically perfect, is one at least that in itself is flawless. But the Greek temples that house the Mitsubishi Bank, the Mitsui interests and the Land Bank of Japan are not in keeping with the spirit of Japan, do not belong in their setting that embraces pine trees floating in the mist quite as much as smoking factory chimneys or printing press.

The builder of the new hotel did not seek to adapt ancient Japanese architecture, surviving now in shrines and a few other buildings, to modern living conditions, but rather to express in modern architectural form the same organic beauty that had found expression centuries ago in Shinto shrine and Chinese palace. He gave Japan an example which she might well have followed in solving this difficult task of reconciling utility with beauty in her modern buildings.

The architecture of Old Japan is a thing of beauty when at its best, with its high roof beam and severe simplicity. The architecture that the Japan of other days borrowed from China has enriched the charm of the islands. For many centuries Japan found her small buildings of wood and plaster and bamboo, tied and dove-tailed together, sufficient for her needs. Here and there was erected a palace or a castle modelled on the style of China with tall towers of white topped by winged roofs that rose one above the other in graceful ascending tiers of flight, but for the most part the Japanese were content with the flimsiest of structures, with tiny houses and shops of thin unpainted wood, roofed with gray tiles of baked earth or thatched with rushes and dried cedar.

The architecture of the feudal castle and the Buddhist temple are capable of adaptation to modern needs and of construction in the fireproof, earthquake-proof materials that this age demands. This has been done in some few buildings; they give promise of what might have been, of what might yet still be.

If Tokyo had but followed this plan in the Government structures built, building or to be built on the hill that flanks the Imperial Palace it would have given the world a unit of beauty that men would have come far to see. The massive gray stone walls that enclose the palace grounds with their white watch towers and curving, graceful roofs strike the note that should have been followed. The whole of Government Hill could have been wrought into an harmonic poem of Japan's past with a Diet building of Mediaeval Asiatic architecture at its crest, an architecture echoed and re-echoed down the terraced sides to shita-machi.

The street that leads eastward from the Imperial Hotel past the palace grounds still has possibilities of becoming one of the most magnificent streets in all the world, possibilities that will probably never be realized. It is broad, and curves just enough to break the barren monotony of mathematically straight lines. Drooping willow trees line it, and on one side the gray stone walls of the palace moat rise from quiet water, crowned here and there by fantastic watch towers of purest white and covered with pine trees whose branches dip down to kiss the silent moat. By night the fairy lights of the Imperial Theatre find their Narcissus-reflection in the long stretch of water that lies like the surface of a silvered mirror, or, if the breeze but stir it, breaks the golden glow into myriad points of dancing light. The cities of Japan might so easily be made beautiful; but are not.

In the costumes of the people, like the buildings, the tourist meets with keen disappointment. He sees many wearing the kimono and straw sandals, but the kimono are for the most part of dark materials. Children and school girls may wear brilliant reds and blues, but no married woman would consider any but the most sober costume. Black silk with a delicate stencilled tracery in white bamboo, pine needles or the blossom of the plum is as far as she will go. That is an acquired taste, and, as one lives in Japan, one learns to appreciate it. Not so the visitor. Only the geisha, seldom met in public, allow themselves to revel in gorgeous color and elaborate kimono and still more ornate obi.

The Japanese encountered on the streets or on the railway trains stare at the newcomer as a Fiji Islander in native dress would be stared at in the West. The tourist has expected to look at everything in Japan with curious eyes, but he finds the Japanese even more curious about him. Because it is a simple, child-like curiosity and therefore not impolite, no effort is made by men, women or children to conceal their interest in the stranger from over the seas.

On the surface, the great cities of Japan hold but scant attraction for the eye. The newcomer is certain to be disappointed. If he be so fortunate as to leave the cities behind and strike boldly out into the open country, there is another tale to tell, for no Lafcadio Hearn with words and no Japanese artist with brush or chisel has sketched with such unerring beauty as has

Nature itself with mountain and mist, pine and bamboo and terraced rice field, moss-grown rocks that border a waterfall or swirling stream, or some ancient shrine sheltered by tall cryptomeria and camphor tree.

And if the tourist remain in Japan long enough to cease being a tourist, the drab cities, too, reveal their beauties to his widening vision.

Tokyo offers him the satisfying simplicity of the gray stone wall and placid waters of the palace moat, or the glorious mingling of sound and color and life that throbs through the narrow streets and paths of Asakusa Park.

Other cities have their hidden beauties, a treasure trove for him who will but search them out.

Beneath this pattern of strangely mixed beauty and depressing monotony, underlying and pulsating through it, is the true joy that Japan may offer to the stranger—the charm of Japanese life and thought. At times it is repellent, and the foreigner draws back to blaspheme the islands of the East, and again he sees in the hearts of the people that which attracts and wins his admiration; perhaps his love.

It is difficult to grasp both phases, to evaluate them properly and to come to a conclusion that takes both into consideration. More often, only the bright and joyous side is seen; and Julian Street writes a book. Or only the ugly and repulsive is discerned; and John Paris produces "Kimono." Both are right; both wrong. A true mirror of Japan would show reflected bits of both, and the reflected picture must be judged as a whole and not by any of its details alone.

Young Japan

YOUNG Japan is thinking, but its thoughts wander. Young Japan is discontented with the grip that the powers of the past have on the nation. Young Japan —and not age in years but youth in thought makes up Young Japan—is in rebellion.

The standard that has been raised is Liberalism, a standard to which thousands are rallying in this Island Empire of the East. But the design and the pattern of the standard are not clear cut. Young Japan wants greater liberalism in government and in other walks of life, but Liberalism is a very vague idea to most of Young Japan, which is striking out blindly at what seems substance but may prove only form.

The Spring Equinox

THE voice of many Buddhist bells, deep-toned and sonorous or with a lighter, tinkling rhythm; the measured clack of wood on wood; the murmuring of ancient sutras; outside the warm moisture of a gently falling rain—the Spring has come.

All of the last week and through today the temples of Japan have welcomed pilgrims. Ten thousand daily have prayed before the Kwannon in that temple which now stands where thousands perished in the fires of earthquake. This eastern part of Japan, this section of the nation then drank sorrow to the full, and to the millions left the Higan must mean much. So many, many souls have passed into the Great Beyond, through Higan, to Nirvana.

It was good that as the dawn broke into springtide there came rain. The warming rain of March and April is welcome to the dry soil of Japan that so seldom thirsts. It seemed a promise for the coming season of plenty.

Nyubai, or the Rainy Season

THE air is gone. A cloying, heavily sweet dampness fills the space between the earth and the thick upper reaches of the great cloud banks against which the June sun beats as it forces the growth of all green things, for the nyubai is Nature's hot house. In its blanket of warm moisture the bamboo and the bullrushes shoot to their full height; moss creeps out of crack and cranny to cover stones and wooden water pipes and temple walls; the warmth, the rain and the rich black soil conspire to make this world a luxuriant mass of green, green foliage and of brilliant blossoms glimmering through the rain.

The blue of summer sky is gone, for overhead is a gray solidity of watery clouds which trail their damp, filmy garments over the face of land and river while their thin, thin fingers break through the surface of the earth to caress and nourish bulbs and roots in which lies hidden the glory of the out-of-doors.

In this thick, misty dampness we live and move and breathe. The murky warmth which quickens life in plants melts men. From somewhere far above to somewhere far below, earth, sea and sky are blended; the three elements have fused into one vast band of dark, gray, throbbing stillness that fills a space within the universe, while men drift listlessly through mud and wet and heat.

Sunshine and Summer

THIS is the season of childhood in Japan, and Japan is the land of little children. There are festal days scattered through the calendar in which children play their part. On the third day of the third month comes the O Hina Matsuri, the Festival of Dolls, for the little girls; and on the fifth day of the fifth month there is the Boys' Holiday, when great paper carp float from tall masts of bamboo above each peasant home that boasts a son. The Birthday of the Buddha is in early April, a day for childhood, and even the Christmastide that is now returning to the East from its Western shelter is becoming more and more of a joyous, happy season for the wee tots who wear kimono. But these days are all more or less formal and are very fixed. They come slowly, it seems, and they pass so swiftly and are gone.

It is the summer that is the true season of childhood in Japan, as I suppose it is in every land, the time when their hearts are most carefree and happy. It is ushered in by the tinkling wind-bells that delight the eyes and the ears of the child, by the call of the vendor of ice cream and shaved ice that taste as good to the youngsters of these islands as to the children of Western lands, by the trilling of birds and the blossoming of flowers, by the throwing wide of wooden amado and paper shoji that have barred the out-of-doors away all wintertime in order that the season may now flood into every home in the land.

The sun pours down, and the grown-ups swelter, but the sunshine is all sunshine and not heat to the myriads of boys and girls who play about the dusty streets or in the green parks of the cities.

In the pools and lakes of these parks and along the embankments of streams and rivers and tidal canals the bare-limbed children paddle about in full enjoyment of the water. Baseball, the sport of Young America, is quite as much the sport of Young Japan, and a neighborhood nine of boys none of them nine years old will be a seen lustily playing the game and shouting in childish treble: "Strike one!" or "Ball two!" or "Atta boy!" They do not know the English language, but they do know baseball lingo, and its language is universal wherever the game is played.

The semi will soon be with us, the singing insects which the Japanese delight to catch and house in tiny, delicate cages of bamboo, listening through the twilight hours to their weird, elfin songs as the Westerner joys in the golden outpouring of the canary's throat or the more liquid, silvery music of the nightingale.

There are professional dealers in semi, but a semi bought can never be prized as is the one which is caught. The children rush about carrying long, slender poles of bamboo, the tips of which are daubed with sticky bird-lime. But let a cricket or a katydid or any other "musical" insect make its presence known, and the swaying end of the bamboo descends upon it. Its wings are entangled in the gum and in a few seconds it has found a new home in one of the wee cages.

The semi is sometimes hurt, sometimes sorely bruised, for there is an unthinking cruelty in the child-mind that bodes ill for all tiny creatures that come within its grasp, but usually it is carefully guarded and protected until it can be placed within its miniature cage where its song may be enjoyed by all the family of the lucky youngster.

It is not always the semi which the children chase with their shouts and laughter. Around the iris-bordered edges of some placid pool they gather, called there by the brightly fluttering gauze-wings of brilliant dragon flies which hover above the quiet water or alight upon the spears of green bullrushes.

Down the street there comes an itinerant seller of queer toys, and the children swarm about him as he pauses in his passage, slipping from under the flexible shoulder-pole and letting his two bundles of trays or great boxes rest upon the ground. Curious little contraptions that are a delight and wonder to wide-opened childish eyes are shown. They will not last for long, once wee fingers find them, but while they last they give an innocent pleasure that many who have grown older would re-grasp if they but could—if they but would.

Perhaps it is a pedlar of sweetmeats who is the Pied Piper of Hamlin for the moment, or a coolie-merchant of ice cream. Little fists with tight-clenched coppers thrust upward to receive the goodie that is his exchange gift.

In the homes of the wealthy with their spacious gardens there is happiness among the children, too, but they are barred from the careless playground of the streets and parks. A tiny lady walks demurely by her mother's side over graveled paths. The soft colors of her summer kimono are like unto the wings of a butterfly; a widespread parasol of paper makes of her the blossom of a morning glory swaying gently in a passing breeze.

This is the season of childhood in Japan, and Japan is the land of little children. In parks and on the streets, in temple courtyards and in the secluded gardens of the rich, in city and throughout the countryside the summer burgeons forth with birds and flowers and trees and happiness, but the loveliest blossoms of the summertime are the laughing little elves who scamper here and there in sheer abandon to the call of the great out-of-doors.

Flower of the Buddha

WHEREVER the teaching of the Buddha has swept in, there will be found the sacred flower from which he sprang in miraculous birth.

Here and there in the islands that make up Japan a vast covering of pink and white and green upon the surface of the waters spreads in wide glory in the month of August, but more often the lotus of Japan are to be found in smaller clusters. Priests of the Buddhist temple, set deep amid its grove of stately cryptomeria and brooding quietly in the semi-silence, semi-twilight of their shadows, have cut away the trees and made a miniature lake with island, bridge and all that the garden of a temple should contain. There in the brilliant sunshine that falls on this single spot that lies open to the skies the cupped petals of chaste luxuriance serve their Lord and Master.

In the mountains of the islands where hillsides slope more gently and so form a little valley for the work of peasant men and peasant women will be found an acre or half-acre of these lovely blossoms, bounded on all sides by the sun-imprisoning green of rice that is nearing harvest. Even in the dirty, dingy cities of the Empire there are spots redeemed and glorified by the color of the blossoms of the lotus.

"The Pines Are in Their Glory"

OUT of the cloying city and into the beauty of the countryside of the Isles of Sunrise! Away from the dusty streets with their congestion of motor cars, trams, bicycles, pedestrians and confusing traffic of a diversified nature to the Tokaido and the Nakasendo and all of the roads of ancient Japan, whose well-trod stones echo to the footsteps of villager and farmer pacing the little distances encompassing their lives.

Near the great ports and cities of the Empire the human stream that pours along the narrow roads is of far more interest than the thatched houses and rice fields that are passed, the orchards and the little fields of grain. There are farmers coming into the city to sell the work of their hands and backs, and there are equally as many going out with their profits or carrying the gifts of the cities to their homes. There are ox carts, hand carts, 'rikisha, burdened shoulders and a few horses being led slowly along with straw canopies arched over them while their half-dressed leisurely masters walk in front, wielding a lazy fan in the blaze of the noonday sun.

Farmers and farmers' wives stand knee deep in the muck and water of the rice fields, stooping over to give care and attention to the tender plants that will insure a full harvest at the season's close. Here and there a half-grown boy treads a water wheel, his monotonous work lifting the water across low embankments from one field into another. No machinery as known to the farmers of the West is seen, for farming in Japan is still a matter of the hands and of the most primitive of implements. The golden rape and the pink clover, with frequent patches of barley and millet, grow on little squares of ground raised above the level of the canal-threaded rice paddies, while long ridges bear diminutive mulberry trees whose green leaves form the food of silkworms kept inside homes that possess an opening near the eaves.

In season, young girls move among the tiny trees of tea, dwarfed to a foot or so in height, that cover many hillsides. With their great baskets of woven bamboo and wearing white and blue towels over their black locks they raise the song of the tea pickers, singing the words that came from the lips of their mothers and grandmothers and for many generations before that:

> The pines are in their glory
> With branches spreading wide,
> And needles fast unfolding
> Here by the riverside.
>
> Peace reigns within the Empire
> The fields abound with tea,
> Foreshadowing for our rulers
> Days of prosperity.
>
> Famous the Bridge of Uji,
> Famous the tea prepared
> From the under-flowing water
> For the ancient feudal laird.

> Like lovers in their wooing,
> The fireflies at night
> Illumine the thick darkness
> With softly glowing light.
>
> No need for further singing;
> Here is the final word:
> Let joy swell up within us
> And make itself be heard.

On along the coast or up into the mountains that tower from the sea, and the scene changes. Little villages and farming hamlets scattered through the mountains or nestling by the banks of some life-giving river in the rice country retain the quaint customs and simplicity of other days. The pressure of an evergrowing population and of intensive agricultural development is seen in thousands and thousands of homes that crowd one another along the roadside through the fertile lowlands, and in the diminutive holdings of each farmer.

The song of the Japanese nightingale breaks from a thicket of bamboo and the noise of men is stilled to listen to the flood of melody. Far ahead gleam the mountains of Japan, the vivid green that breaks at their base sweeping upward until it pales into a dull blue that is redeemed by the glittering purity of the white snow that etches the peaks against a still bluer sky.

Peasant girls with their outer kimono tucked up and showing scarlet, green or yellow skirts beneath lower their paper umbrellas as a motor car rushes by, scattering mud and water to right and left in spite of the futile mud brushes that the law of Japan insists must hang from each hub cap. Children, pursuing dragonflies with long slender poles or singing the song of some childhood game, throw up both hands in salute, perhaps shouting "Banzai!" and grinning at the strange visitors from the cities and beyond the seas.

The depressing grayness of unpainted buildings is offset by the ethereal beauty of mists and mountains, of whitecapped waves that break in spray against the shore, and the still, blue waters of deep lakes, by the sunshine that dazzles as it strikes the snow-whitened cone of Fuji, the greenness of trees and fields and groves of bamboo or the majesty of cryptomeria, by the glorious colors of the cherry blossoms or wisteria or the iris blooms. The ugly and the beautiful; the new and the old; the toil and the pleasure—the life—of a people and a nation!

The Mountain Top

FROM the little inland station the broad pathway leads, with here and there a gentle curve, to the base of the mountains. In the month of April cherry blossoms line the road, and in the autumn there flames the scarlet of the delicate tracery of the maple leaves of Japan. In June, when the iris bloom, the roof-trees of the peasant homes must be sheer lines of beauteous color, made brighter by the contrast with the weather beaten thatch beneath the purple flowers. And through the year, in spring and summer and in all the months, the waters of a clear mountain stream, curbed now by little walls of stone, cry out in bubbling accents of the mountain home from which they come.

Stone lanterns, showing traces of the earthquake tragedy, stand along the merging of the road into a mountain trail. Tea houses, a small temple, clustering groups of 'rikisha men and pilgrims tell the tale of a well traveled path.

As the damp earth, trodden smooth by the feet of thousands but still showing the sharp marks of wooden geta, takes the place of white gravel road there sweeps from the heights of Takaosan the clean breath of the semi-sacred mountain, pure and sweet and cool, refreshing to the city dweller worn by the dust and noise of a constantly rebuilding capital. Giant cryptomeria rear into green arches overhead, their brown trunks forming a long colonnade mounting ever upward. The deep shadows, flecked here and there by the dew dappled sunlight, pricked by the white and purple of tiny wild flowers, silvered by the baby stream that laughs over little rocks undreaming of the water wheels where later it must serve and labor, enfold the pilgrim and the merry-maker alike and impart to them a bit of the great silent calmness of the Buddha whom they honor.

The road climbs up and ever up. Carven stones, gray and lichened with the passing years, are scattered along the mountain side. Pilgrims, with their legs bared to the warmth and with the banners of their homes across their shoulders, toil onward. Two men, half nude, bearing great burdens of faggots on their strong backs, are descending from the steeps. The mountain road is filled with a ceaseless stream of humanity, of humanity that laughs and joys, that weeps and lives and dies, that climbs the heights of rapture and sinks back into the pleasant, easy valley with its cherry blooms and maple leaves but without the majesty and awe of cryptomeria.

The group of temples on the crest, red and gold and brilliant lacquer covering the finer artistry of the wood carver, is like a glimpse of Nikko and its splendour in this mountain fastness farther south. Bronze lanterns with the temple crest guard the broad steps of stone that lead to a wide terrace overlooking many valleys winding toward the sea. A great monastery rambles over space, the home of priests and temple acolytes and pages. The deep boom of the temple bell, high in its scarlet home, sounds through peace and silence unbroken otherwise save for the crunch of wooden sandals on the gravel, the murmurings from out the temples, the chatter of the many, many pilgrims.

In the most resplendent of the temples, in the one that is flanked by guardian angels or by guardian demons made of bronze, a mass is being said, A family has gathered there, kneeling on the soft creamy mats of clean rice straw. The grandfather, the son, the wife, the grandchildren; the priests in vestments of the Buddhist Faith; the temple ornaments, the image of the Buddha: These are the contents of this gorgeous, carven testimony of men's faith and belief in the Divine.

They can not be a family of great wealth, they who have gathered here to honor their dead. Their own clothes are but cotton; the priests are not robed in silk. Nor are the chanters of the mass the elder priests. They are but boys, the acolytes and the young students, with shaven heads and eyes still fixed on the wonders of this life.

The incense curls into the air and floats across the terrace into space. The bells ring in a sonorous, monotonous rhythm of eternity. The boyish voices intone and drawl the words of ancient India. The family bows in reverence. Surely if anywhere Heaven lies closest to the mountain tops.

One in Each Generation

THE terrace on the high hill with its ancient trees and its stone embankments and its deep well are not for me, the foreign guest within the Empire of Japan. The owner, who is a descendant of one of the most noble of Japan's families and whose wife has in her veins the blood of Emperors, intends to build there a home for his crippled sister, she who carries in her twisted body the curse that was pronounced by dying lips on the great family and on its unborn descendants more than three centuries ago.

I had left my little house by the shores of its tiny lake and had wandered over the nearer sections of Yamanote, on the highlands of dusty Tokyo, searching out a spot where I might build a home. And I found the terrace high on the crest of the hill.

There had been a house upon it once, but it had long since disappeared. Only the broken stone steps and the well and the weed-filled garden told the tale. Tall trees, like the forest oaks of England, stood guard, while beneath them were marshalled in uneven array the bamboo and the cherries and the pines. An unkempt arbor of wisteria half-veiled a little Shinto shrine that was the abode for the spirit of some of the noble family long dead and gone. The breeze from the south swept over the housetops in the valley below, and the wind from the north would come in winter, broken only by a barrier of swaying bamboo. To the east the terrace looked out across more gray rooftops to the blue waters of Tokyo Bay and the green islands built so long ago to guard the city from the invading Westerner. It was a most lovely spot, where one could sit and dream, where one could build a home and rest contented.

But the Marquis had set it aside for his poor sister. He was courteous, and he regretted that he could not let the foreigner have the half-acre of secluded hillside woodland in the midst of the dust and grime and ugliness of a rebuilded and rebuilding Tokyo, but it was for his sister.

The Marquis' name is not one that creeps into the newspapers when the cables tell the story of the day's political events. It is enough for him to spend his time as the gentlemen of Old Japan spent theirs, in composing poetry and viewing the flowers or performing the stately and elaborately simple tea ceremony. His life has been a happy one, whether colorful or not, for he wooed and won in the days of his youth a princess of the land.

His family is one of the proudest in all Japan. Many years ago, more than three hundred, the scion of his line had saved the life of Hideyoshi, of the Taiko, of the great warrior who laid the basis for the establishment of the Tokugawa Shogunate and who united the warring provinces of Old Japan into a nation.

As the Taiko lay sleeping in his Kyoto palace one night, a political assassin who was also a mesmerist crept into the palace and cast his spell of sleep over the retainers guarding their lord there. Gently and scarcely breathing, the assassin stepped over these prostrate bodies. Nearer and nearer he approached the inner chamber where the Taiko lay. But soft as were his footfalls they were sufficient to set in motion the delicate golden feathers of a chidori, of a little incense burner in the shape of an albatross. The golden feathers jingled, jangled, one against the other, and the Taiko was disturbed in his sleep, and he called drowsily to his faithful retainer, to the samurai-ancestor of the Marquis.

The call of his lord and master was stronger than the spell of the mesmerist bent on taking life. The samurai sprang to his feet, saw the intruder and grappled with him. For minutes on end they wrestled back and forth, falling again and again across the bodies of those still under the magician's charm, until at last the loyalty of the samurai triumphed over the evil of the assassin, who lay spent and panting as his victor triumphantly bound him with silken cords snatched hastily from the palace walls.

He was condemned to death, the assassin, condemned to be boiled alive. He, too, was loyal to his master, the mortal enemy of the great Hideyoshi, so loyal that he chose to die in agony the ignoble death of a thief, for he insisted to the end that he had come to steal the golden chidori and not to kill the Taiko. He insisted thus so that no other might be implicated in the plot. But as he died he called on all the Gods to witness his curse on the samurai who had captured him and on all of his family to come, imploring that in each generation one of the proud family should be born maimed.

The Gods heard the prayer and they granted it. From the day of the Taiko to this, one of the family has borne in his body the mark of the curse of the dying man. Some have been lame and some have been deaf or mute, but always one has been forced to pay for the life that went out in pain so many years ago, more than three centuries ago.

And so, the terrace with the giant trees and the well and all its wild, unkempt loveliness is not for me.

The Marquis, who is wedded to a princess of the land, is to build there a retreat for his poor sister who can not walk by herself and who has never walked since the day of her birth and who never will walk, even unto the day of her death.

The Mountain Spat It Forth

A REPORT as of a thousand guns breaks on the air. The homes and shops of Karuizawa were deserted as the villagers rushed out into the streets. Shading their eyes with their hands, they gazed upward toward Asama-yama, for they had learned from many years' experience that such a thunderclap of noise meant the volcano was once more in erruption. Who could tell when it might send forth a shower of ashes so heavy or a stream of lava so great that they would have to flee down the narrow valleys to the coastal plain?

They gazed upward, but the mists so common to Japan veiled the great mountain with their haze, and not even the customary spiral of smoke could be seen arising against the sky.

In the morning we took the little narrow guage train from the village of Karuizawa straight up into the mountains behind it. Up was the only direction in which it did go straight, for the roadbed wound and curved like a coil of rope as it steadily ascended toward the clouds. The flat Karuizawa plain, itself almost a mile above the sea, stretched below, its green fields and forests, its red and white and neutral tinted houses forming a rather untidy array that increased the pleasure of a glance at the flower covered mountainside, for the azalea, the wisteria, the paulownia and the fragile mountain cherry blooms were in their full glory in the high mountain air despite the word "June" glaring from the calendar.

On up the little line of steel crept, its own path seeming scarcely more than a strand of rope. A beautiful waterfall and turbulent mountain stream are passed, but a great part of this mountain land which lies idle is not unlike the rolling, windswept plains of Texas and could be used to vast profit for the grazing of cattle. It could be farmed with upland crops, in all probability, but certainly it could be used by cattle breeders to good advantage. Today it is an idle spot in the heart of an overcrowded Empire.

The crest is reached, and we cross from one province into another, soon puffing to a halt at Jizogawa, our destination.

Here Mount Asama is only four miles away, and the great terrace upon which we stand stretches to its base in a unbroken line. Mountain carpenters, busily at work constructing a new home and burning charcoal, tell us first of the erruption of the night before and point to a thin coating of fine ashes on the new boards, ashes which came from the crater of the volcano. Then we lift our eyes to follow theirs to the mountain top, where we see, standing erect on the bare ridge high above us, a giant cylindrical rock, apparently about thirty feet high and five or six feet thick.

"Last night with a terrible roar Asama-yama spat it forth," they say without emotion.

The Politician

HE haunted the cafes of Tokyo each night, the cafes that were poor imitations of the West, and the far more lovely restaurants that were pure Japanese. He preferred the modern cafes, for there, when the beer had been flowing for an hour or so, a democratic fraternity of all the guests prevailed. In the subdued, aristocratic restaurant indigeneous to these Isles of Sunrise even vice takes on a dignity and a seclusion. Adventures are to be had, but they have to be searched out, arranged for in advance. There is never, almost never, the luring enticement of a chance encounter and an absorbing aftermath.

Well-groomed, so well-groomed as to be overdone, pussy and puffy-eyed at forty, he did not realize that his measure was taken at a glance by all save the most unsophisticated; and with them he would not waste time.

He was a politician out of office but not out of a job. Because he had been in the West and knew the ways of the West he could make friends with the Westerner, could always tap his party's treasure chest. His job was to make friends with the foreigner in Japan, with the diplomat and the journalist especially, and win him to a sympathetic frame of mind toward his political party.

Night after night along that street in Tokyo that

is a Japanese contorted version of a Gay White Way he passed up and down. All the cafes knew him as did all the waitresses. Some of these modern girls of a hybrid, changing civilization welcomed him with smiles and words of pleasure, some with downcast eyes and hearts filled with trepidation.

He would drop into a vacant seat beside a vacant table, order his beer or whisky or, if there were young Japanese nearby before whom he could preen, a cocktail.

Then he would cast his eyes around the restaurant, searching for his evening's prey. He had to earn his living, of course, and every foreigner he bagged was chalked up to his score by party headquarters which blindly, foolishly believed that the party thus made friends with all the world and that, once in power, London, Washington, Paris and Nanking would think all well in Dai Nihon.

The foreigner, interested in this strange world in which he found himself a stranger, responded kindly to the English words of this friend-seeking Japanese, although he felt a strange repulsion. The conversation grew, and in a few minutes the two were seated at the same table. Drinks were ordered, and the Japanese would not listen to the plea of the foreigner that he pay half.

With quick, unthinking questions the foreigner would ply his acquaintance, seeking to know something of the life about him. More interested in Japan than in this one Japanese, he forgot his first distaste for the overdressed fop.

Never forgetting for a moment that his business

was to bag a foreign sympathizer for his political party, the Japanese sat back and studied quietly, cruelly, analytically his latest victim. He sought to detect the weakness and the strength, the likes and dislikes, of this chance-encountered opportunity.

Once he felt sure of his convictions, the party henchman subtly set about to attack the foreigner at his weakest point. It might be liquor, woman, art, desire to know men with big names—any of an hundred of the foibles of mankind.

A keen psychologist, he would seek out the unprotected spot and then bombard it or sap a slow weaving course toward his goal in the manner of trench warfare.

Usually he achieved his aim, but in his very victory lay defeat. Able to dissect the character of others he failed utterly to understand the repugnance which he himself provoked in them. His blinded party believed in his efficiency and value merely because he could meet and talk with foreigners. But, where that party might have found a latent friend, he made an active enemy.

Propaganda has become an ugly word and a still uglier thought. If ever it has been personified, wrought into the body and the brain of a living being that all might see and shrink back from it in sickening disgust, that person is the party henchman of Japan who, spider-like, haunts the cafes of changing, charming, hybrid Tokyo seeking ever for the foreign prey by which he makes his living.

A Gift for a Gift

TWO little bits of lacquer they were, two tiny giftboxes, one bearing the crest of a Prince of Japan and the other the signature of that English lady in the now distant day when she had, in defiance of tradition, instructed the little Prince and his brothers in the way that school lads are taught in England. And the English lady and the Japanese Prince had each given the amah a pair of lacquered gift boxes, tied with silken cords of red and white, hers with her signature in gold scrawled across its surface and his with the simple crest of his proud family painted on it.

The amah was holding them up, two little boxes, half of the treasure which meant so much to her. She was offering them to an American who had since come across her path and whom she had served as faithfully and as well as ever she served Prince and teacher. They were her gifts to the American who was now leaving, the greatest gift she had to offer. She was sharing with him the honor that had been hers.

She was repaying a debt, for that American had done a thing which touched her deeply. When first he had come to Japan he had sent back to America, back to a little golden-haired neice, a kimono and geta and paper umbrella and Japanese doll and all the things that are dear to the heart of a child in Japan.

And the little neice had sent from America to Japan, had sent to the amah in distant Japan, her photograph and the word that the doll had been christened with the name of the amah.

It was hard for the amah to part with the two little boxes of black lacquer, but the effort it cost her was a loyal effort. She was of samurai blood and her father had served in the cause of the Tokugawa, but the Restoration had brought poverty and death, and the amah had somehow or other to support an infant brother and so had taken service in the household of a Prince of Japan. She was of samurai blood, and the obligation of a gift for a gift, of a heart-beat for a heart-beat, was strong upon her. There was no questioning, no faltering.

It was hard for the American to accept this tribute of a grateful heart, but when a sacrifice is voluntary to forbid that sacrifice is cruelty.

Two little boxes of black lacquer they were, the gift of a Japanese Prince and an English lady to a faithful servant, and the gift now of that servant to an American because kindly consideration has not gone out of the world. The gift of an American to—surely the future will not let the two little emblems cease to carry on their mission of happiness and sympathy.

The Hakone in Winter

A BRIGHTLY lighted train whose dingy blue plush seats are crowded with kimono-clad men, women and children rushes through the fast gathering gloom of a heavy snow storm. A change to a tram that slips through the slushy streets of the coastal village of Odawara and into a narrow gorge of the Hakone Mountains as it begins its long climb upward; a second change to a more sturdy car that zigzags up steep precipices and through long tunnels in the early night, and the three of us disembark to plough through drifts of snow to the warm hotel at Kowakidani just before the old year dies.

In the morning the strong sunlight streams through the bay window and we rise to greet a world of crystal white, glistening in the gold of the first sun of the New Year.

From Kowakidani, which is the Lesser Hell, the road slopes up the side of a mountain, rising curve on curve until the crest is topped. On the left a wonderful valley lies stretched below, lengthening but narrowing as we climb higher and higher, aided by our long staves. The road passes through dark evergreen forests whose branches bear a thick burden of pure white snow. At each vantage point a little tea house is perched, a half-dozen children in front scrambling about in the snow or rolling it into a great image of Dharuma, their Budhist Saint. The road winds high and higher; the valley dwarfs as the mountains tower upward. A dip in the road brings the hot springs of Ashi-no-yu, a slight rise follows and the crest is passed.

On the left are the tombs of the Soga brothers with their devotional offerings; on the right are the twenty-seven images of Jizo carved by Kobo Daishi eleven hundred years ago. A few steps farther, again on the left, is the great Jizo cut from the mottled black face of the high cliff.

Another stretch of snow covered road, a curve is rounded—below lie the silent waters of the Lake of Reeds, the promotory crowned by an Imperial Villa and a few huts clustering along the shore. Across the lake and through a gap in the pine-clad hills the white glory of the Sacred Mountain catches the gold of the morning sun and by the alchemy of its ancient magic breaks it into myriad diamonds as the quiet lake in adoration mirrors in its purple depths the beauty and the grandeur of O Yama.

"*Blows the Cherry*"

> Isles of Blest Japan!
> Should your Yamato Spirit
> Strangers seek to scan
> Say—scenting morn's sunlit air
> Blows the cherry wild and fair.

As the gold of each April dawn breaks through the mists of the east, thousands of the tender cherry buds of Japan burst into the glory of bloom to add their delicate beauty to the pink clouds that enfold the Empire in this month when the world is young; with each summer-bearing breeze there drifts to the earth a shower of myriad pink petals.

The single cherry blossom! Yamato Damashi, the Soul of Japan, here finds visibly expressed its exquisitely beautiful culture, its simplicity, its loyalty to the August Mikado and to the gods "who dwell on the Plain of High Heaven," its Oriental acceptance of the ever-present and not-to-be-dreaded death, and its joy in the delicate fragrance and perfumed glory of Nature.

Motoori, leader of the historical school, whose Shinto-samurai firey faith in the divinity and sanctity of the Imperial House helped lead to the downfall of the Tokugawa and the restoration of temporal power to the Emperor Meiji, put into words the heart of his people when he called on the stranger to look on the wild cherry scenting the morning sunlight.

The plum, emblem of virgin womanhood, blossoms while the snows still whiten the brown earth of Japan, but when the cherry trees bloom the whole world is once more putting on the garment of sheer green that breaks at the base of Fujiyama in allegiance to the snows that are eternal on the sacred mountain.

Along the banks of the moat between the British Embassy and the gray walls of the Imperial Palace there is a tunnel of pink blossoms mingled with the green of graceful willows; lining the sweeping drives of the high plateau of Ueno Park hundreds of kenbutsunin—flower viewers—stroll about or sip their amber sake; on the broad stretches of the River Sumida the light tinted blossoms are reflected in the restless water flowing toward Tokyo Bay.

All Japan is en fete. As the thousand and one cherry trees of Tokyo, of Kyoto, of Nara and the Tokaido break into misty clouds of pink, the toil and burden and the cares of life in this Empire are forgot, and the Japanese are once more the children of Jimmu Tenno in the days when the land was young and the gods were close. Trooping forth they go, by the thousand, by the million, for the cherry blossom season is at hand and nothing else matters. A storm may come tonight and the fragrant beauty be shattered; today is the joy of life.

Up the Sumidagawa go the boats. Barge after barge moves slowly and gracefully on the waters of the broad stream, each decorated with lanterns, flags and gay banners. Even more gaily decorated are the crowds they bear, for in the time of the cherry flower the dress of every day is laid aside for bright colors and grotesque masks. Here is a barge laden with geisha dancing on the prow in bright sunlight; there a multitude of schoolboys raise both hands overhead in salute as their clear-voiced "Banzai!" floats across the water.

Up the Sumidagawa to the Arakawa. The river's bank is lined with colorful boats moored to gray jetties. The broad acres of the Arakawa resort and its green dykes are swarming with the happy mummers and the whole world is in love with the joy of the season. Sake, samisen and dance all blend to perfect the one time when the Japanese loses himself in the spirit of pleasure.

In Kyoto the multitude of temples is embowered in the pink blooms that bend lovingly to kiss the sweeping roofs and the majestic columns that are the visible triumph of Buddhism. The stately white or soft brown of a severely simple torii glimmers through the pink of cherry, the soft green of the willow or the more sombre green of the pine. The Miyako O-dori, the Great Dance of the Home of the Mikado, imprisons for a fleeting moment the beauty of the blossoms and transforms it into the grace of motion.

When Nara became the first true capital of Japan, at the time that Alfred the Great was uniting the Angles and the Saxons, the beauty-loving Japanese went each spring to view the cherry blossoms. In the "Time of Peace" they reveled in the glory of the pink and white blooms. The great Taiko rebuilt a temple and hung the fences from Momoyama to Daigo and those around the cherry clad hills with silken curtains for his flower-viewing guests. It was not the gorgeous double blossom that the Taiko and the Japanese loved, but the single bloom, "as simple as a country maid," for the fourteenth century priest Kenko wrote that "the double cherry is an oddity, and so exaggerated and eccentric that it should not be cultivated at all."

The cherry blossom season grows in swelling beauty from morning to morning. Spot after spot in the Isles of Sunrise is transformed by the glory of bloom. One night the sun goes down, a rain or wind rises, and day dawns once more.

The pink petals float on the surface of the little lakes. The ground is carpeted with the tiny, soft leaves. The clear air is filled with the fluttering beauty of color as the blossoms yield their lives, for their time of glory and their mission is fulfilled.

"The cherry flowers, too, have their seasons of blossoming and fading. What is there for the Japanese soul to regret in death?" The samurai bowed his neck to the sword to pay forfeit with his life for the life of the Frenchman he had killed to "prevent the defilement of sacred Japan."

> In this world of ours,
> Soon the blossoms fading fast
> Lose theit dainty tint;
> Though they have no colors gay,
> Hearts, too, change and fade away
>
> —Ono-no-Komachi.

> Fickle hearts of men
> Soon are blown away, ere yet

Shaken by the breeze;
Cherry blossoms, you will find,
Scatter only in the wind.

                —Ki-no-Tsurayuki,

The beauty and the wonder must fade and pass. They must bow to a higher force.

The samurai must give his all for his Emperor; he, too, may then yield his life.   Yamato Damashii!

But though the blossoms pass, they come again each spring in still more glorious beauty. And this is repeated again and will still be repeated again and again, from the days of now unto the forever.

Year after year
The fair Yoshino's cherry blossoms
Bloom in the spring; however
Can we see the flowers;
As they are hidden dormant in the parent branches.

At Noon

THE noon gun sounds and Tokyo knows the sun has reached its zenith for that day. In the factories of Shibaura, Kawasaki, other districts where men work with iron and steam, with delicate machinery and with the cruder pick and shovel, all labor ceases as they gather round to chat and chaff and dip their chopsticks into the rice box of Japan that takes the place of the Western worker's dinner pail. Work ceases for a time for almost the whole nation.

In the schools the children rise from their low desks to march outdoors and start homeward. At Sukiyabashi near the center of Tokyo's business district with its congested traffic there stands a proud policeman, striving to direct with waving arms a stream of bicycles and motors and pedestrians who do not understand the rights of others to the public streets. The children pour from out a school nearby, a school for youngsters who have just begun to learn how difficult it is to read and write the language of their birth. They are little tots of five and six and seven years, dressed in blue uniforms with knee pants that hang far below the knees, their books in black satchels strapped across their tiny backs like the knapsacks of the soldiers of the Empire. They are laughing little girls, garbed in kimono with wide flowing sleeves, perhaps with an incongruous white apron in the Western fashion draped across the brilliant colors that they love.

Out of the schoolyard and into Sukiyabashi they pour, a bright stream of color and of happy, carefree childhood. Even the dangers of the traffic at the busy corner hold no terror for them, for they know a friend awaits them there, that the strong arm and the all-conquering, awe-compelling gestures of that friend will part the flow of traffic as the Red Sea parted once to let the children of Israel pass through.

As they near the waiting black-coated figure wearing a tin sabre their pace quickens, and they run with little cries to cling to the hands of him who waits. They cluster about him, the boys in their dark uniforms like little moths, the tiny bits of womanhood like butterflies who have broken from the chrysalis. Majestically and with the impressive pomp of the law which he so proudly represents, the policeman raises one arm to stop the traffic from the east and west. The children break away and scutter across the tram lines to the safety of the tiny park across the street. Now and again the policeman takes one tiny tot by the hand or swings a little girl on to his shoulder to walk across the danger spot in company with the children whom he guards.

The noonday crowds stand still, the rush and bustle of the hour is stopped, and for a few seconds the blundering traffic of Tokyo is actually controlled, controlled not by the policeman but by the little children seeking safety on their homeward path.

An Overcrowded Empire

"AN overcrowded Empire."

It is a phrase descriptive of Japan that has been used so often it has become trite.

Figures in books and graphs and charts mean little to the mind untrained to such statistical data. Of what real use to most of us is it to read percentages of population, acres that can be tilled, the average number of square feet allotted to the average man?

The senses are more to be trusted, the sense of sight, of smell, of sound. If less scientifically accurate, still they are more intimate, an actual part of life, and the testimony that they bear is infinitely more convincing.

A long road stretches from the capital of Japan to Kyoto and now on to the western port of Kobe, a road that once played its part in history but that has fallen into disuse with the coming of the railway.

The Tokaido it is called, the Eastern Sea Road, for it lies as close unto the shores of the Pacific as the mountains and the jagged littoral of the island will permit. Some times it dips down to be kissed by the more daring waves that dash against the rocks to cast their dying spray upon its weathered stones. Again, it swerves upward suddenly, sharply, cruelly, to surmount some star-aspiring mountain range. Flat patchwork fields of gold-green rice at times embrace it, the Tokaido shooting through their midst straight as an arrow or winding like a summer breeze, raised with its majestic border of tall trees above their mingled mud and water that the sunset's afterglow turns into a glorious mirror of pale pink.

Whether along the coast or through farmlands, the Tokaido swarms with a never-ceasing burden of humanity.

Low houses with overhanging eaves of time-blackened thatch line both sides, and a thousand, thousand, thousand children dart from wide-opened doors into the roadway. In every home is glimpsed the housewife, a baby on her back, another one or two or three clustering about her knees.

On the road itself there passes from the sunrise till the sun goes down a ceaseless stream of workers. Men bent double drawing little carts, others bowed beneath the weight of huge burdens carried on the back; children playing; women working—an overcrowded Empire that the eyes may see and believe.

Only in the high lonely mountains does this pageant of humanity fade from sight. There, the very solitude, the lack of human habitations and human beings, serves but to accent by its strangeness the congestion of the regions where men can scratch a scanty living from the soil by patient labor.

In the densely people cities there seems scarce room to breath. Thick-crowded houses with the tiniest of gardens stand with roofs interlocked. Millions of citizens pass up and down the narrow streets, and all so near together that it is impossible to proceed but at the common pace. Everywhere, on every inch of ground, are men and women, children; people.

In the heat of summertide, as the evening falls and breezes from the ocean sweep in with freshening breath, houses are deserted and the thousands swarm into the parks and to the promenades. Within the confines of the capital they seek out the Ginza first of all.

There may have been a time when it was possible to enjoy the cooling breeze along that street. If so, that time has gone. Solid buildings and sun-reflecting pavement have played their part, but most of all must be blamed the throngs and throngs of human beings.

So tightly packed are they, shoulder to shoulder, breast to back, that crowded heat is generated.

At the corner of Owaricho, busiest spot in all the Empire, four white-clad servants of the law seek to control the traffic. A whistle blows, an arm is raised, and down the center of the street there pours a stream of motor cars and clanging trams that is as nothing when the glance turns toward the sidewalks. A solid wall of straining, sweating men and women sweeps past on both sides. So must it have seemed to the Children of the Lord when the Red Sea parted for them, for the drops of water that were held in leash could have been no more numerous, no more densely packed, contracted, than are these human beings.

Each April, when the universities disgorge their graduates, there begins the heart-rending search for employment. There are too many applicants. There are not places for them all.

Nor is it only among the educated that this overabundance of hands and brains is to be found. In the lowlier walks of life two men or three divide the work that should be done by one.

In the village home or in the poorer districts of the cities as the time for sleep comes on the millions stretch themselves to rest. Lucky indeed are they who possess more than a single tatami, more than one mat but six feet long and three feet broad, for sleeping space upon the floor.

In every room of nearly every home they lay them down to rest, so many in so little space that there is little chance to toss about and not tresspass upon some sleeping neighbor's domain.

And in the graveyards of Japan, builded upon the hillsides that they may not encroach upon the rice fields of the living, not even the full length of a worn body is offered to the dead.

Burned into ashes or crumpled up into sitting posture with locked arms and legs, these men and women who have not had space enough while living are still more closely packed in their long sleep. A foot, two feet, in rare cases even three feet square, is all of this earth's surface that is vouchsafed them for eternity.

Why bring statistics, tables of comparison, figures for mathematicians and for the academic to bear upon this problem of an overcrowded Empire?

The senses—inaccurate, unscientific, more to be trusted—tell their tale in brain-searing accents.

The Priest Is Dead

 E—tern—i—ty! E—tern—i—ty! E—tern—i—ty!

 THE West knows not the rhythm. Only the disciples of the Buddha could know it, could have evolved it.

 E—tern—i—ty! E—tern—i—ty!

 The sonorous, deep-toned throb of the drum pulsates through the air. Its accents, measured and slow, a different measure from that of all other lands, all other religions, strike the ear and heart.

 The priest is dead. The young priest, he who tended the lake and the garden and the candles before the altar of the Buddha, is no more. Nay, he has passed upward, along the Wheel of Life, along the Karma that binds each until perfection is reached and we sink into the finite infinity of All.

 E—tern—i—ty! E—tern—i—ty! E— the drum has ceased!

 From the throats of the disciples rises the chant. The rhythm changes, but it is still the rhythm of eternity. Slow, sonorous, in minor chords—what do we, children of this century, know of life and of eternity? Words can not tell, but the slow-beating rhythm, the continuous pulsation of that Buddhist chant before the altar breathes it, tells it, lives, it; lives it in death.

Toshogu

EVEN the drabness, the grayness, the dullness to the eyes of weather-worn Tokyo can at times be lovely and can add their bits to the beauty of life. There are places and moods, there are moods that belong peculiarly to certain places. One of these is the mingled Shinto Shrine and Buddhist Temple of Toshogu on the high plateau in North Tokyo that is Ueno Park.

It is a winter afternoon, an afternoon of the Season of Great Cold when all the trees are bare and all the grass is dead, for the plum blossom promise of the coming spring has not yet been stirred to life. The brief sun is already enshrouded by the haze of deadened clouds that all day have threatened snow. The very heavens have taken on the sombre hue of sleeping earth. Gray and green are the colors of the misty isles of Japan, but this time of year the gray alone is dominant, insistent, triumphant in its all-pervasiveness.
The crowded, dusty streets of the colorless city, a monotone of dullness, have been passed through to reach this spot. Filled with a squirming mass of men and mechanism, the threading of these byways is a veritable battle with Fate. For many minutes the battle is fought, and then the strident motor car purrs up a little slope, into a broad avenue lined with bare-limbed cherry trees that overlook the lake below with

its sere stalks of what in August had been a glory of the green and white and pink of lotus blossoms. Beyond the lake, in the mist and haze of the horizon, rise the hills of Hongo, the square tower of Dai Gakko jutting upward. On down the avenue, over the crunching river gravel rolls the car, to stop short at the torii-guarded entrance of Toshogu.

There are ghosts here, the ghost-spirits that have loved Japan too much and have refused to leave it but cling nebulously, wraith-like to the places that they knew when life was full of color, battle and ambitious dawn. Overcrowded though Japan may be with the living, the myriad spirits of past heroes and past peasants, the souls of the men and women of the centuries that are gone, are everywhere. Up and down the old Tokaido they throng noiselessly. In farmer's hut and in the palaces they make their homes. About the temples, shrines and green mountainsides they cluster in their silent communion with the seed of their loins who still walk this earth with heavy bodily tread. Ever present, ever ready to respond to loving heart and knowing brain, these spirit-ghosts of Michizane, Yoshitsune, the Taiko and all others offer an austere and mystic friendship to those who in so short a space of time will join their ranks.

The stone torii arches over a pathway paved with well worn slabs of dull lava leading straight unto the temple-shrine. Lanterns, darker gray than the mist-clouded skies above, stand in long rows along the path like the broken columns of some roofless temple in Old Greece. Above them bare, leafless branches scarcely stir in the quietness of the late January afternoon. A strip of barren ground borders the dried grass of a dead summer.

The many-lantern-bordered path runs true and straight to the closed gates of the sanctuary, to the sheenless gates of time-dulled crimson lacquer that are barred by a simple rope of rice straw with its fluttering paper offerings. Each lantern was tribute of some daimyo to the Tokugawa in the days when the Shoguns of that line held unchallenged dominion throughout the length and breadth of the Eight Great Islands.

Every daimyo, every samurai, every commoner in all Japan touched reverent forehead to the ground in deep obeisance to the Tokugawa then. Proud in their might and glory, the Shogun and the Shogun's sons wrought for the future. Here, on this high plateau in the northern part of their capital and stronghold, they strove to duplicate the greater temple in Kyoto that an earlier Emperor had accorded fame. Here, in their well-protected Kwanto, they built up a power that was invincible. To the temples and the shrines they builded on this spot they brought a son of the August Mikado, holding him as honored hostage that, no matter what might come, they could never be branded as disloyal to the Imperial line.

Their power rose and waxed. The gorgeous temple-tombs of red lacquer grew in number with each generation. The forced tribute of the daimyo added to their visible glory. Great indeed were the mighty Tokugawa, supreme, unchallengeable.

The crest was reached and soon the downfall came. Clansmen to the south and west, nursing their hatred for two centuries and more, grew louder in their mutterings. All the scheming, all the planning of the Tokugawa came to naught. The Emperor in Kyoto, not the Prince Imperial in Ueno, was the man-god to whom the people turned.

Here on the heights in Ueno, here amid the gorgeous temples and the giant trees, was the battle fought to recover the person of the Prince, to scatter and demolish the retainers of the Shogun.

Blood and battle, the clash of swords and the heroism of warriors—all was fruitless—all was ended.

These are the ghosts who whisper silently to the loving heart and the knowing brain that drifts, too, along the lantern-bordered pathway this gray afternoon of dank midwinter, drifts past the gate with its scars of battle, drifts half-walking and half-dreaming, living in today and yesterday as one.

Faded grandeur, faded glory, days of old that have not vanished linger lovingly along the pathway bordered by the sacred tribute of the lords of shore and mountain to their master and their ruler when the sword, the bow and arrow fixed the destiny of all the islands that lie nearest to the sunrise.

The soft grayness of the winter skies, the bared branches of the trees, the lifeless grass of the past summer form the warp for this brocade of Old Japan. Lanterns of gray stone that are never lighted, walls and carvings whose vermillion, gold and azure no longer glow and glitter like the flames that once they were but still half-reveal the fire in their hearts, trembling through the ashes of the smokeless burning of decay, make the woof of this visible, intangible texture woven first by haughty Shoguns but redeemed, toned down and modified by the master-weaver of aesthetic beauty, by the hand of Passing Time.

Shot through the warp and woof of these grayed and deadened colors are the threads that give it soul. Here a touch of Shinto, a single naked thread of color, gleams out against the drabness, unable in itself to give color to the whole. Many threads of history are interwoven, but they are in the subdued tones of a nation and a people whose whole history clusters 'round their tombs and temples, battles fought hand to hand, and a subjugation to a higher power than self, a half-rebellious abnegation before the desireless Buddha.

Only Buddhism, only a Buddhism modified by the Shinto sons of Dai Nihon, could have created this place.

There are places that provoke the moods that are their truest tribute.

When the Dead Return

FIRED into flame by the spark that springs from flint when a blow is struck, the dried hemp seed that has been placed before the portals of the homes of those Japanese who honor and obey the slightest command of their heritage from the past will blaze forth tonight into a signal light for the souls of those who have passed beyond and are struggling to attain Nirvana.

O Bon, the Great Festival, which is sometimes called the Lantern Festival and sometimes the Day of All Souls, and sometimes the Feast of the Dead, is ushered in this evening with the lighting of these signals to guide the spirits of all ancestors back to the hearths of their children and grand-children and descendants unto many generations. For three days the spirits of the dead and the living will commune, will feast and will make merry together. And then once more the wavering torches at the doors will spring into life and tiny boats of straw will be set adrift on the face of the waters, laden with sweets and sake and other offerings and ablaze with the flames of candles for the comfort and sustenance of those who sleep beneath the waves. This second lighting of the signal fires is that the spirits may see to wing their way back whence they came to dwell for this brief period with those who later are to join them.

All of the Kwanto, all of Eastern Japan, which flaired with a more lurid and hideous flame as summer passed into autumn one hot September noon, so few, so many, years ago, will glow with this gentler light for the next three nights. There are so many, many souls in this corner of the world who will be coming to celebrate O Bon as honorable guests, so many, many who needs must have the path which they now are to follow pointed out clearly to their wandering and disembodied spirits.

In the drab port cities and the garish capital of Japan, where the Way of the West is all too often followed rather than the Way of the Gods, the compromise that Japan has made with modernity extends even to the honoring of those who sought with all their strength to preserve the ancient usages and prevent the ingress of the "barbarian." There will be electric bulbs rather than fires of hemp seed before the creaking doors of some of the crude shacks of corrugated iron and scrap timber, of mansions of brick and steel and concrete, that stand today in lieu of the delicate grille work of wood, weathered to a soft brown or a dull gray of other years. It is even whispered that in the homes of some no beacon torches at all are to be touched into flaming light.

Away from the Marunouchi buildings with their tale of progress and of utility, away from the steel rails that carry monsters breathing smoke and filth that settles in tiny spots of soot on creamy mats of rice straw, away from the strange mixture that has daubed the Eight Great Islands during the past half-century, the tale will be different.

In the high mountain tablelands and along the island studded coast of the Inland Sea, on the peninsula of Boshu and in the Province of Idzumo, wherever the Old Japan still dominates, O Bon, the Feast of the Dead, which is sometimes called All Souls' Day, and sometimes the Lantern Festival, will be observed with all the elaborate and yet simple ritual that has come down through the long years since first the Emperor Shomu paid Imperial homage to his forbears in this fashion.

The crescent of homes and temples and graveyards that climb the hills of Nagasaki will be pricked out by tiny sparks of light as the guiding signals are kindled and as those who live in that city of the south troop forth with samisen and biwa, with sake and with cakes and fish, climbing the winding pathways to the multitude of spots where lichen-covered blocks of stone mark the resting places of the dead, there to place their lanterns of the O Bon and to commune and to make merry with the souls of those who have returned to rejoin for three days the children they have left behind.

On the third night, as the Great Festival ends, the living will move down the hills again to the water's edge to launch on the waves their little boats of woven straw, bearing a flickering candle and laden with the good things of this life, that the many who have no grave other than the ocean's bed may also be comforted and sustained by the homage of the living.

There are many details of the ritual which must be faithfully observed. There must be a horse of straw but eight inches high, and there must be a cow made of eggplant, and there must be another eggplant that is white and has a living branch attached and there must be many another offering before the family Butsudan. And there will be, scattered here and there throughout the Land of Fertile Rice Fields, the Bon O-dori, the Dance of Rejoicing for the Souls that have been liberated from the Boiling Pot of Hell.

It is a dance that is seldom danced these days, the religious folk dance that held Lafcadio Hearn entranced for hours as the darkness of the third night of the Feast of the Dead wore into the glory of a dawn that crept over the misty hills and mountains of the Province of the Gods. It is a primitive dance, and that which is primitive is elemental and does not always measure up to the standards of nicety that this civilized age has set. And so, now when the girl workers in a factory on the very edge of Tokyo dance the dance that their sires and grandsires danced, it is modified to suit the wishes of the rich factory owner.

The story of the Bon O-dori is told by a Buddhist:
"When the mother of Mokurensonja, one of the disciples of the Buddha, was sent to Hell and thrown into the pot that forever boils, Mokurensonja descended into Hell and offered the prayer of Issai Kyo at the edge of the boiling cauldron. Slowly the lid of the seething pot began to rise, and it ascended into the air, so that the souls of many who were within besides the mother of the holy monk escaped from out of the boiling waters, and the happy souls clapped their hands and danced around the rim of the great pot to express their great joy.

"And from that day it became the custom of the living to mingle their joy and to dance with the souls of those who are delivered from out of the boiler of Hell on the last night of the Bon when the lid is raised, and we call that wild dance of rejoicing the Bon O-dori, or the Great Dance of the Feast of the Dead."

The Spider

IN Japan, one should kill not a spider after dark; the belief is far, far older than any man now living.

That first summer, two great spiders, black and hairy and jovially ugly, span a shining web from where a corner of the tiled roof dips in a graceful curve to the needles of the pine whose branches droop across the placid lake. The strands of silvery silk that made the web were few. They glittered in the moonlight. In themselves—they were beautiful. But always there obtruded the thought of the great spiders, hairy and black and jovially ugly, that had woven those fairy cobwebs from their own bodies.

The summer passed.

The nyubai came again, the period when earth and sky are blended in one vast mist of moisture and man breathes not air but some other damp and cloying element. Again the spiders threw their silver stands from blackened, dripping eaves to green pine needles. That summer, in the dusk, while yet the western sky glowed with the flaming passion of a day so glorious that it sought still to live, one spider died.

It was not death, but murder.

One should not kill a spider in Japan after the

sun has courtesied below the mountains of the islands.

The summer passed; the victory of the autumn leaves gave way to magic purity of snow; the plum, the cherry and the willow brought the spring; the nyubai came again.

The web once more extended to the shores of the little lake, to the pine that no longer stood quite so tall and straight. At night, just as the daylight faded into dark, the fragile silken skeins of silver trembled. Across them passed a single, round, black, hairy body.

There are moments when loneliness and silence become a tragedy.

This time the death was merciful; not murder.

In Japan, one should not kill a spider after dark.

A Saint at Peace

IT is a long and leisurely walk from the populous part of Kyoto to the Honen-in, which nestles close against the base of Higashi-yama toward the northeast. It is a walk of beauty.

A path that one may take if one wish and know it winds in and out of temple gardens, under stone torii and across bridges that arch the running water brought from the mountains for a thirsty city. There comes the moment when Niyaju-oji is reached. Beneath a bridge of stone the clear waters flow rapidly yet quietly on their way. Young maples touched with the delicate green of April stretch along the bank, scattered in among the great clouds of floating pink that are cherry blossoms, and the breath is caught in joyous wonder at the beauty of this revelation.

A vagrant breeze blows down the mountainside to claim its toll, and the air is filled with the fluttering color of their myriad petals. They seem to be themselves an element, for the elements have changed from earth and air and water, fire, and what else, into color, into the blue of sky and stream, the pale green of the awakening earth and the delicate pink of the fluttering shower of blossoms.

On around the base of Higashi-yama winds the narrow roadway, past homes and shrines and shops, the tree-clad mountain rising on one side and the gaze sweeping out across the plain in which Kyoto has been builded as the eyes turn leftward. The poets and painters of ancient, semi-ancient, days sought out this curving mountain slope, here to build the simple, little homes in which they joyed. Their ghosts still walk the paths they loved, and the poetry of a vanishing age seems now to mingle in the fragrance of the springtide.

Giant cryptomeria guard the gate of the Honen-in, one of the tallest trees leaning out in friendly protection across the stone-paved entrance path. A thicket of fairy-like bamboo shuts off the public road, while the pines and cryptomeria tower upward, shrouding all in a soft, dignified gloom. Always in the month of April the scarlet blossoms of the camellia lie scattered on the path of stone and on the dark, damp earth which flanks it. "Like the heads of warriors fallen in battle," the crimson flowers rest at random on the earth. Moss covers all the rocks and trees, for the sunlight scarcely creeps into this pathway with its gentle rise that leads to the temple. Blackened timbers set into gray granite form the archway of the retreat which beckoned Honen Shonin when his exile was recalled. It was here that he found peace.

A little hut he built, a hut where he could rest his head and dream until Nirvana called him.

The saint and teacher could not thus long find tranquility, for from the mountains and the plains, the seashore and the riverside, there flocked a multitude of followers, disciples. His hut became the center of their new-built homes.

When Honen Shonin's soul took flight there rose

this temple where his dwelling place had stood. It is home and shrine, a mingling of the two, both in appearance and in spirit, as should all true temples be. No sect, no organized religion keeps this home for him, but loving tribute pours in from all Japan and from all believers in the faith of the Buddha, just as the people of all varying Buddhist doctrines flocked to the feet of Honen Shonin while he still walked this earth.

The slow-ascending path, shaded, subdued, solemnified, its darkness stained with the scarlet of the fallen heads of the camellia, is fit introduction to the temple-home. It speaks in silent accents, telling the tale of him who wandered searching after truth and finding it so long ago in India, and of his follower in Dai Nippon.

In this temple courtyard simple buildings of white plaster and brown wood border the formal garden with its little lake, buildings of white plaster and brown wood. Two gardens of white sand are combed each morning into formal patterns, and an ancient bell tower crowns a more ancient rock so thickly clad in moss that it seems centuries must have rendered it homage.

In the temple at the rear, the temple that is covered with a roof of thatch and was once a home, a Buddhist mass is being chanted. The dirge-like rhythm rises, falls, resounds as the murmured voices breath the sacred words. A wooden drum and a tiny bell are struck in ceaseless monotone.

On the black-lacquered floor the blossoms of this year's camellias lie in great cone-shaped heaps. They are not placed in formal vases to the right and left of a formal altar, but lie thus in humble beauty, their deep color honored by the polished lacquer which reflects them as a quiet pool mirrors the silver moon.

The service ends, and the doors are opened wide that the worshippers may make obeisance to a small shrine to Shakya Muni, founder of the Buddhist Faith, which is just across the narrow garden, carven from the hillside.

Sunlight enters here, falling on the path of stones and on two mounds of sedate white sand that flank the temple steps.

There is sunlight in the garden, but the hillside shrine to which all bow in reverent supplication is still shrouded by the shadows of the cryptomeria, still lies wrapped in the sombre tonelessness that the Teacher sought and found.

His disciple, many centuries later in an alien land found peace and deep serenity also, found them in this retreat where they still hover close, tangible and yet unreal, sensed and felt but no more to be grasped and catalogued than is the scented vapour of the burning incense drifting from the temple altar out across the sunlit garden to curl and cling about the silent, shaded hillside shrine.

Coast and Criff

FROM the tree-embowered shrines and temples and the decaying, moated castle of gray stone that nestle in the dingy fishing town of Odawara, the coast line of Japan sweeps south and westward in a great half-moon of jagged rocks and cliffs where the mountain range that gave birth to the beauty of O Yama drops down in swift, precipitous descent to touch the sea. Here is the home of earthquake and volcano, of storms that lash the waves to fury and of sulphurous springs that boil from out the earth to spread in crystalline form the salts of the nether region in a great display of ashy desolation that contrasts most vividly with the swaying, lithe bamboo, the dark green pines and the dull sunshine of the orange trees that edge this bit of Hell. Out to sea there rises on the air the column of white smoke that ascends ceaselessly from the cone of volcanic Oshima. The majesty of the Great Mountain in its sublime indifference to this world of men and little crawling creatures who tremble with the shaking of the earth rears over all. Earthquake and volcano, steep mountain and a storm at sea—the narrow shoreline at the base of the Hakone should be a region of terrific grandeur, awe-inspiring terror, desolation of the quality that would have been a solace to the heart of Poe.

Grandeur there is, and sublimity in spots, but

these are dominated, overcome, subdued by the picturesque, the glory of sheer color and the softening touch of growing greenery that creeps over what was wasteland, droops in graceful tendrils to conceal the gashes in the face of stark cliffs where great blocks of rock have been chipped off, and welcomes Wordsworth rather than the gaunt Virginian of such haunting unhappiness.

The mountain stream that tumbles down to join the sea at Odawara is but a narrow band of pure, clear water save when the melting snows of springtide or the storms of summer flood its wide, rock-strewn bed from dyke to dyke to leave still other giant boulders lying in the valley. Across a long span of steel the railway creeps to enter into mountains which it has been skirting. Mile after mile the trafficway winds in and out these mountains, now deep in their cold darkness, now emerging from the tunnel to plunge across a slender tressel bridging some smaller torrent or to purr smoothly over the safe niche in the face of a cliff that has been carved out by man that he may traverse with ease and speed this land of beauty which Nature has not yet quite yielded to his dominion.

The sea lies far below, its deep blueness breaking into a lacery of white as waves strike the tiny strip of golden sand that fringes the towering, weather beaten rocks. Terraces cut out or built up in the steep slopes are covered with the glossy leaves and fruit of gold of sweet, sweet mikan of Japan. Rice fields are rare; they are the product of the tamer stretches of the coastal plain. Bamboo and pine; the scarlet of the maple and the straight, naked, sturdy trunk of the paulownia; the pale blossoms of the cherry tree in April and the wild blaze of brilliancy with which the azalea cover hills and mountains when their season of blossoming in turn arrives, are to be seen.

Across a deep valley rolls the train, a valley that is green with verdure but that once was only raw, crude earth of broken mountainsides, for it was here at Nebukawa that "the mountains walked to the sea" in that stark, tragedy which came one hot Stepember noon.

Only a roof or two was left projecting above the blanket of transplanted soil and rough boulders under which the village died.

The train runs on to Yugawara, to Atami, where it now passes under the great mass of the whole Hakone since the engineers have completed their bording of the mountains.

If one be wise, the train is left at Yugawara for a tramp along the road to the hot springs of Atami. The road, too, clings close to the face of the cliffs, as they tower upward on one side and drop in sheer descent to the foaming breakers on the other. Along this road there moves a stream of travelers on foot. Students out for a gay lark, old women with bent backs and children carrying burdens to and from the town, here and there a pilgrim with his little bell and garments of soiled white all trudge along, some with song and laughter, others careworn and weary. Workmen tied to the trunks of trees by long ropes for safety are tearing down the hills and filling in the empty spaces.

The battle of mere man against great Nature goes on ceaselessly, triumphantly.

The great half-moon of jagged rocks and cliffs, of bamboo and of flowers, of thatched huts of peasants and the ugly shacks of workers by the day curves out into the sea. Like a strange jewel it embosoms distant Oshima whose smooth sides sweep upward in lines to the crest of that island-volcano. A cloud of smoke boils up into the sunshine to mingle with the clouds of mist.

The day is ending and the sun drops out of sight. The blueness of the sea deepens and the lines of Oshima turn to gray but are pricked out in sharp relief by the pink and salmon and the saffron of the eastern sky that catches a reflected glow of color and of beauty from the horizon of the west cut short by unseen Fujiyama. The cloud of smoke, too, takes on the tinge of a peach blossom.

Slowly this darkness creeps up and up, the sharp edges of the distant island-mountain wavering into dusky mistiness until at last only the ascending smoke is seen.

The shadows of the cliffs have mingled with the shadows of the night; the greenness of the trees has darkened into blackness; the sun has veiled its face and the sound of breaking waves below seems to grow sharper and more distinct, while a distant temple bell is heard as if to make up with harmony the loss of sight.

The Desire for Friends

HE will never speak the first word, the Japanese who is host in his own country. If the stranger from out the West, who must remain forever guest in these islands, a man apart, not of Japan, but once break through this reserve the response is instantaneous and as warm as the pleasant touch of spring sunshine.

He would be friends, the Japanese, friends with the foreign guest within his homeland. His desire for friendship is so eager that at times it is pitiful, and yet his training, inheritance, something within him makes it impossible for him to make the first advance unto the foreigner unless he has been coarsened by overmuch contact with the West.

He will sit implacable and with motionless features on the train or elsewhere, side by side with the foreigner whom he wishes with a child-like passionateness to know. Not a glance nor smile, not an indication of any sort gives evidence of this desire. The foreigner who does not know and understand is frozen also into an unnatural icy reserve by this surface attitude, and so often fails to bridge the gap that he alone can bridge.

Yet if he but say a word, but make the first approach, the Japanese beside him will respond as to a long-known friend.

Depreciation of self and apology there are on his part—such are the manners on his people—and praise for the homeland of the foreigner. In broken English or, if the foreigner must speak in the language of the land, in still more broke Japanese the friendship grows and ripens as do plants in the hot rainy season.

Questions and answers are exchanged, questions that would be impertinent if one did not understand the innocent sincere simplicity of curiosity in Japan. The Japanese retains his dignity yet renders a touching respectful homage in his evident regard for the foreigner and for foreign ways.

In no land are all men worth the knowing.

At times the friends thus made become a burden; more often they strip bare, to him who cares to see and sense, the tremulous soul of the Japan that is emerging into its dream-inspired future.

The Modern Mecca

HE was a student, a young man from the country to the north of Tokyo who had been two years in the capital and must stay another four to obtain his university degree, but then he would return to his home at Morioka. "I do not like the city," he said. "I belong in the country, and it is to the country that I wish to return. It is shizuka; Tokyo is not."

He was one of only three young Japanese whom I have met who were not lured to Tokyo as by a siren. Up and down the islands, in the smaller cities and in the remote countryside, every Japanese, or certainly, every young Japanese, desires to go up to Tokyo, believing that there lies opportunity and a brilliant future. It was a relief to find this lad of a good family who preferred the charm of the rural districts; but it was surprising.

One night I took him with me to dinner, and we went to a restaurant on the roof of one of Tokyo's new office buildings. There is nothing of Nihon-no-Funiki, of the Atmosphere of Japan, at that restaurant. The atmosphere is that of New York, rather than of Tokyo. It is not quite New York, to be sure, but it is more like New York than Tokyo.

I was anxious to see what reaction my Japanese friend with the love of the countryside in his soul would have toward this bit of Western atmosphere that is far better done than most of the imitations in his country. His eyes gleamed with pleasure and he uttered a little exclamation of delight as this luxury unfolded itself before him.

"Is this really like New York?" he asked, not once but several times, and then, reassured that it was, he said: "I want to go to New York."

Since that day he has been studying English most assiduously and is planning for a business career in the greatest business mart the world has known.

Some time, perhaps in his old age, he will retire to Morioka, but all his thoughts, all his ambitions are now concentrated on New York.

And he is but one in how many millions!

The Children

"GOOD-BYE! Gooda-bye! Gooda-bye! Iijin San, Gooda-bye!"

The short street, perhaps three hundred yards, that leads from the front gate of the little house to the main street with its clanging tram line swarms with little children. They clatter about in their wooden geta; boys in dark blue garments tucked up to free their bared brown knees and legs play good American baseball; little girls play the games their mothers and grandmothers and great-grandmothers played, and many, many of the youngsters scamper about with a smaller, bald-headed brother or sister riding serenely on their little backs.

The narrow lane that turns at the corner is dingy and brown, for weatherbeaten walls enclose it, but it is clean, clean in the way that all Japan is clean. There is dirt, but it is a clean dirt, and the children who play about in it are clean also, all save their noses. The drab, wooden walls are broken here and there by wooden grilles that slide back to admit the children or to let them pour forth. Through the grating is to be seen the clean, bare, yellow interior of the true Japanese house, the mats gleaming and a single painting or the characters of a short bit of poetry forming the sole decoration for the paper and plaster walls.

A few of the houses have a tiny garden plot in front, but most of them open directly on the street, for these neighbors are not wealthy.

It may be because the children have no garden of their own that they so love to come into Iijin San's. In groups of three or four they slip quietly around the house or down the steep steps that climb the little hill. Now and then they come in greater numbers, but not often. They circle the lake, staring at the red-gold carp and perhaps attempting to dip up a few of the myriad pollywogs that wiggle about near the shore. Nothing is harmed; almost nothing is touched.

Out on the street the children fill the narrow channel of traffic as soon as the sun comes up, and the little boy who is apprenticed at the green grocer's diminutive shop is the last figure moving about at night as he slips into their grooves the amado of wood that make of the shop front a blank wall.

I do not know the games the children play. Some of them, a very few, are familiar. At the New Year every boy has a kite and every girl a battledore and shuttlecock. Some of the battledores are wondrous to behold, for on the under side they may have the face of a Japanese actor, a face made of painted silk and wadded until it stands out from the light paddle; the hair is natural. When the girls' festival comes on the third day of the third month I know that the little girls have their displays of dolls, but I do not see them, for the Japanese doll is not to be bandied about but takes her proper place in the niche of honor that is in every Japanese house.

There is one game in which brightly colored cards are thrown to the ground with great force. There is another which is much like hop scotch. There is still another which requires only four hands for its playing and which affords much happiness to the little geisha, who are supposed to be grown up. Baseball, the sport of a sport-loving country, has found a welcome in this land of Sun Rise.

Sometimes a pedlar will wander in the street. His coming is announced by whistle or drum. He will pause, slip from under his long shoulder pole and let his two boxes of toys or his great counter of brilliant gewgaws rest on the ground while the children gather around.

Again, it may not be a seller of toys but a vendor of Japanese sweetmeats or colored ices, and the children who have a sen troop out to purchase a bit of sweetened mochi or dry rice cakes, while those without the necessary bit of copper stand around, their widened eyes fixed on the precious sweets which are not for them.

The voices of the children are raised as they rush about at play, but from the thirty or forty or fifty little throats there does not ascend such a volume of sound as would be heard in America or England.

They are happy, smiling all day long, but they are not exhuberant as they would be in the West.

Happiness is shown by smiles rather than by loud, careless laughter.

"Merry Kurisumasu!"

IT was the first Christmas in an alien land, in the temple-home of a Buddhist god, under the folds of a Shinto flag.

"O Hana San," the amah was told, "Christmas is coming, and the children who play in the lane outside must be given a taste of the greatest holiday in America. We shall buy a tree and a few presents and many golden mikan and perhaps some candles, if you think it safe, and have the thirty children who live nearest come in on Christmas morning. But Motoko San and Sachiko San and Steve San must be among the thirty."

And so O Hana San and the three Ijin San planned their Christmas. The tree was bought and placed in one corner of the dining room, and on Christmas Eve it was trimmed with toys and the candles and the mikan and the candy figures of Daruma, who is a god loved by little children in Japan and of whom they build images from the snow.

The night at ten o'clock O Hana San told the thirty children to come in the morning. She had not told them sooner, because she feared the invitation would be passed from child to child and perhaps guests would come from as far away as the Gate of the Tiger, which is near half a mile away.

In the morning two more Ijin San were in for breakfast that they, too, might see the children and the Christmas tree, and while still at breakfast one youngster came rushing in, wearing his nightclothes, as he had not waited to dress for fear he would be too late.

The front yard began to fill with the children, each dressed in best kimono and each holiday bent, but each very shy, for this was a strange thing, this being the guest of the Ijin San. And then the shoji that make the walls of a house in Japan were thrown back, as the sun of that bright December morning was warmer than the pot of burning charcoal.

As the shoji were opened, the children began to troop in. There were thirty, there were forty, there were fifty. They began to fill the adjoining room. There were eighty, there were ninety there were an hundred and thirty, and the house could not hold them all, so that some had to stand in the garden, since in Japan the shoji and amado that make the sides of a house can be lifted out and then house and garden become one.

Then O Hana San, in a few words, told the children that today was the birthday of the Great Teacher of the Ijin San, just as April eighth is the birthday of the Buddha, and that the Ijin San honored their Teacher by the giving of gifts to others.

The Ijin San stepped up to the tree and began to cut down the presents. The children crowded around, and each one wanted all he saw, but there was no pushing and no shouting and no grabbing, for the happiness of the Japanese does not often take the form of boisterousness, and it is seldom they ever forget, even the youngest of them, to hide violent desire. With the candy and the mikan and the toys, there was a gift for each child, for O Hana San had sent out at the last minute and had increased the store that had been bought for but thirty children.

It was then that Motoko San, standing up in the midst of the hundred gaily clad little figures seated on the floor, turned to us and bowed and voiced her thanks. And then O Hana San, first telling them how to say it, had Motoko San lead the rest, counting: "Ichi, ni, san: Merry Kurisumasu!"

A Japanese Home

I SPENT Sunday with my friend whom we shall call Tetsujiro Hara, one of that fortunate and unfortunate group in any country, the educated middle class. Mr. Hara, who is an American university graduate, and I have long been friends. He has had dinner with me, and I have been his guest at Japanese restaurants, but never before had I visited him in his home.

That is rarely done in Japan. The Japanese does his entertaining at restaurants and keeps his home for himself. If, by any chance, a guest should be invited to partake of a meal in the home, the Honorable Interior, as the wife is called, either does not appear at all or else acts as maid and waitress to her spouse and his friends.

Mr. Hara thought I would be interested in seeing the home and home life of a middle class Japanese family as it is actually lived, which was true, and so was kind enough to invite me and to draw aside the curtain.

Besides, he is very proud of his home, a part of which he has recently built with his own hands.

The day was a magnificent one, with brilliant sunshine pouring through the brisk November air and with the snow-capped peak of Fujisan dominating all of Eastern Japan. The cost of living has driven Mr. Hara from the city proper and out into the adjacent countryside, as it has so many of his fellow brain-workers during recent years. A ride by electric train of fifty minutes brought us to a little station on the Musashino Plain, most extensive of the flat places in these mountainous islands, and famed in song and story from almost the dawn of Japanese history.

It is only recently the city dwellers have begun to invade this section of Musashino, and it is still very much as it has been through the centuries. The thatched homes of farmers stand among fields of rice and garden truck; thickets of bamboo surround rustic temples or shrines; here, within less than an hour of the capital, is as bucolic an atmosphere as could be asked. Is it to be wondered that it is influencing these men of the city's offices who flee the metropolis for the country each evening?

It has influenced my friend, and on his little plot of ground he raises all the garden truck he needs, more chickens than he can eat, flowers of beauty and distinction, and now he is to make a landscape garden in pure Japanese style for his aged mother's pleasure.

His house is Japanese but with certain modern modifications. The walls are sliding screens, but they are of glass instead of paper. One room is his study, with bookshelves and with chairs like those of the West. A cellar, an innovation indeed in Japan, has been dug, and in other ways the conveniences of the Western World have been added to the artistry of Japan. Sunshine streams into the house from dawn to dusk, and in summer the breezes from the mountains play through it.

His mother, more than ninety years old and scarce four feet tall, was pottering around the garden as we approached. She hastily fled indoors, for it would never do to greet the Honorable Guest in such fashion. A semi-detached room, flooded with sunshine and commanding a view of the blossoming plants, has been built for her, and there she may be as secluded as she desires to dream and read.

After a few minutes, in order to permit a change of costume, we called at her room to pay our respects. She came out on the little half-balcony that encircles a Japanese house, knelt upon its boards and gave the courteous greeting of Old Japan.

The wife knelt at the door to welcome us, and the maid hovered in the background. They were all a-tremble with excitement, for never before had a foreigner crossed their threshold, and they were most anxious to please. Knowing my fondness for the bamboo, the hanging scroll in the place of honor had been selected with my pleasure in view, and depicted a grove of those slender, graceful trees.

Through the house we went, my host showing me this point and that, and then out into the garden where each flower was examined carefully and the growing vegetables praised. Here was domesticity indeed, the same domesticity to be found in any country, though the milieu differed.

A short stroll through the countryside followed, and we called on some of the neighbors. There was a retired Commander of the Navy, two artists, professors from the universities. Mounting prices in Japan have driven men of this ilk from the noisy city to the more soothing countryside.

The meal, too, had been especially planned, and the food served was such as a foreigner is most apt to like. The chickens, which formed the central dish, were his own, and most of the vegetables that went into the pot were from his own garden. The wife slipped in and out, serving us and seeing that every want was supplied.

The meal progressed slowly, for it was interlarded with much conversation.
My host glanced at his watch, called his wife and asked her to invite his mother to eat now in her own room. But the mother would not touch a mouthful, not until the Honorable Guest had been fed. So was it with the wife. Only when my host and I had completed our repast did the women of the house break their fast.

Much has been written of the "inferior position" of women in Japan, and inferior it is in contrast to the "superior" place that the women of America occupy. But the inferiority is largely one of convention, and there is the same pleasant comradeship and camaraderie between the husband and the wife in Dai Nippon as in the United States. It was plainly visible between my host and his wife; it is equally evident on the trains of Japan and in other public places where men and women are seen together.

The afternoon passed all too quickly, and falling

shadows warned me that I must depart.

    Mother, wife and maid all gathered at the entranceway, once more to kneel low on the matted floor to wish me God speed and to plead for my return.

When One Is Host

THE little mid-Manchurian city of Changchun was gradually awakening to the fact that an international conference between Japan and the two principal Russian Republics was going on within its precincts. There had been no "conference atmosphere," and to speak of the conference to the man in the street or to the shop-keeper was to receive a blank stare.

When a little Japanese bank clerk there asked why all the foreigners were in Changchun, he was told "the conference," but he still looked mystified. He had heard of no conference. It was then he was told that Tsuneo Matsudaira had come to Changchun to represent the Empire of Japan.

"Matsudaira-ko, Matsudaira-ko," he kept repeating. The suffix "ko" means marquis and, although Mr. Matsudaira is not a marquis, the Japanese clerk was on the right track, for the Matsudaira who was there to negotiate with the Soviet is the grandson of one the daimyo of Old Japan. It was unbelievable to the little Japanese that this great man was really in Changchun.

"But where is he staying?" asked the clerk. "In the Yamato Hotel?"

"No," came the reply, "in the Nagoya-kan."

"In the Nagoya-kan!" Again the little clerk was

incredulous. Could the descendant of a great daimyo, of a daimyo whose ancestors had ruled as Shoguns of Japan, be staying in any but the finest of Changchun's hotels?

"But Japan and Mr. Matsudaira are the hosts to the Russians here, and there was not room enough for all at the Yamato, so they gave it over to their guests," was the explanation that came from one who knew something of Japan psychology and courtesy.

"Oh!" said the little Japanese bank clerk, and smiled. The explanation was sufficient.

If courtesy demanded it, "Matsudaira-ko" would be the first to sleep on the street that his guests might be comfortable. That was proper. "Matsudaira-ko" was living up to the best traditions of Japan, to the best traditions of the Japan of the daimyo and of the coolie.

Flux

A YOUNG University student from the country, dressed in cheap blue cotton kimono and heavy underwear, his features showing strength of character and quite the opposite of Tokyo's Haikara San and Mobo, is seated at a side-table in the gaudily decorated Western-style cafe with his father, a smaller man, who is garbed in an ill-fitting suit of readymade clothes from out the West.

They have ordered foreign food and whisky. but the father hesitates when the whisky comes until he sees how his son deals with it, and then treats his own drink likewise, shuddering afterward. Steak, with an accompanying knife and fork, is quite beyond him, and he humbly asks his son how to eat it.

The son reaches over, quietly cuts the steak into small bites, and then takes the first bite himself, showing his father how to hold the fork.

A Stranger

THERE can be no more lonely figure, anywhere, than that of the young Japanese girl educated in and impregnated with the West when she returns, a stranger, to Japan.

Still more tragic, she is forced just now to bear the burden of her own people's desertion of the Past, who look to just such symbols as this girl for their scapegoats.

Faith

HE was aged and bent and weary with disease as he stepped from the 'rikisha. A friend supported him on right and left that he might make the little pilgrimage to supplicate the myriad deities of the Shinto Faith.

Beneath the straight lines of severely simple torii he passed, and slowly made his way along the stone-paved path to the lowest of the moss-covered steps that led upward to the weather beaten shrine. Slowly, one by one and with the greatest effort, pausing after each minute ascent to rest awhile and gather strength for the next climb, he toiled onward to his goal.

The thin curtain of reeds that hangs before the sanctuary was half rolled up, the creamy mats of the almost barren room gleaming spotless as a single shaft of sunlight found its way through dark branches of the cryptomeria to break in a sharp line at the very base of the stand supporting the tarnished metal mirror that the Great Sun Goddess has bequeathed as a symbol of herself to these her children of the Land of Fertile Rice Plains.

The pilgrim reached the topmost step and made his weary progress across stone flags to the half-open shrine. His hands cleansed with running water, he made obeisance to the spirit housed within and prayed to have his heart cleansed likewise.

The Plums Are Blossoming

LIKE the chaste snows which they daringly embrace, a faint scattering of the petals of the virgin blossoms of the plum lay on the ground of the old garden at Atami. It was still the New Year tide but in this spot, warmed by the breeze from off the southern ocean, sheltered by encircling mountains from the chill winds of the north, the first flower of the year in all Japan was in its glory.

The plum blossoms of Atami, sung through the years, the object of a thousand pilgrims seeking beauty, lie in a mountain valley itself hemmed in by kindly hills and bordered by tall pines. The rough, uneven slope of the garden rambles upward, broken into little peaks and ridges, splattered with great weathered stones whose shaded sides are clothed in moss.

There is ever heard the sound of rushing waters from a turbulent mountain stream, crossed here and there by rustic arching bridges, swirling and foaming over massive boulders as it plunges through the valley toward the sea.

A floating cloud of purest white has bent low to kiss the garden. The upper branches of the trees have caught the snowlike blossoms, entangling them until it seems a pearly veil of diaphanous beauty floats like a low-hanging mist over rocks and streams.

The gnarled, gray-black trunks and leafless branches from a colonnade, like unto the black legs of a heron supporting the white-feathered upper body of the graceful bird.

The dried grass of last year's summer is a soft neutral-tinted carpet for the throng of merry-makers, for where the blossoms are there will be found the Japanese in myriads.

Gay laughter and the twanging of the samisen rise from the grass to float upward through the flower-filled air. A snatch of song is heard, a happy call, the chatter and the murmur of the holiday.

Men from the cities stroll through the garden, wearing the bath-kimono of some nearby inn. Little children dressed in gay attire romp beneath the trees. Groups of coolie-workmen, lowest of the low, take pleasure in a beauty that belongs to all the world. The restrained democracy of the Japanese is evidenced, save when some man from out the city and his too-disdainful wife with touches of the West in her expensive garments draw to one side. The geisha of this little coast resort, wearing their bright kimono of the New Year season, forget themselves and act the children that they really are.

From early morning the Plum blossom gardens have been thronged. As the day wears on and noontide nears, the laughter grows more careless. The human hubbub rivals the mountain stream. Sake and beer flow freely, yet more freely. Lunch boxes are brought out and torn paper strews the ground. Here and there someone still true to old traditions brushes off a poem and hangs the fluttering paper with its artistic characters to a blossom-laden branch.

In this little valley, closed save for its one narrow entrance, the sun drops swiftly behind the pine-clad hills. Laughing and shouting or more quietly talking, this group and that stroll out and toward the town. The hegira increases, swelling until the narrow road that winds seaward is choked with the slow moving crowd. The stray, lingering few in turn depart. The voice of the swift-rushing stream again becomes triumphant. The beauty of the blossoms is not gone, but there are none now to see it, none save one student stretched full length upon the ground and seeking with his brush to capture the fair scene that for most must remain mere memory.

Where the fragrance of plum blossoms lingers, where the flowers that defy the winter's snow to give promise of the coming spring break into bloom, there hovers always the spirit of an early hero of Japan, the mystic presence of Tenjin Sama, of Sugawara-no-Michizane.

Driven from the Court of the Mikado by the machinations and the evil whisperings of jealous enemies, this Minister of the Right so long ago looked for the last time upon the beloved plum tree blossoming in his garden at Kyoto as he departed for his distant place of exile. His heart still loyal, Sugawara-no-Michizane picked up his writing brush and gave Japan a poem that has been treasured through these thousand years:

> When the east wind blows,
> Awaken your scent, ye plum blossoms;
> Forget not the Spring,
> Though your master is absent.

In the poetical imagery and symbolism of Japan, these few lines tell the tale of his unbounded devotion to his Imperial master in the midst of his own distress.

Discharged, dishonored, he journeyed south to Dazaifu in Kyushu, scattering a trail of poems as he went that serves still to mark that melancholy journey. Like the petals of the fragrant plum blossoms themselves, these poems of the scholar-statesman form a drifting chain of memory from out the past into the present. The shrines to Sugawara-no-Michizane, deified as Tenjin Sama, also fleck the mountains and the valleys of the Isles of Sunrise like the petals of the chaste, brave flower that heralds the coming of spring, like that beloved plum tree which flew one night from Kyoto to the garden of his exile in distant Kyushu to bear him companionship, for Tenjin Sama has "been restored, doubtless by the prayers of millions, to his former character of loyalist—a gentle, learned scholar with high ideals, who loved the Emperor, the plum blossoms and poetry, and who died a martyr's death, blessing the name of the Emperor—now popularly worshipped as the patron deity of calligraphy and learning."

Ichi Riki

"ICHI RIKI!" The name means much to those who know Japan, who know not only her treaty ports and the strides toward Westernization she has made since the day when the Black Ships from out the Barbarian West dropped anchor off the little fishing hamlet of Uraga for the first time.

The blank pink wall along the main street of the ancient capital of Kyoto whispers not a word of what is to be found within the tea house beloved of the Forty-Seven Ronin. Nor does the entrance passage to the Ichi Riki. It is as the entrance to hundreds of other restaurants throughout the Empire.

Inside the similarity to all its fellows is still preserved. Restrained dignity reigns over the rooms floored with delicately browned mats of rice straw. The walls are sombre except where the tokonoma breaks their plain surfaces with its kakemono and ikebana.

But the geisha are not as other geisha of Japan, nor are the treasures which they bring forth as other treasures. There is the letter that the chief of the Forty-Seven Ronin wrote to the Ichi Riki, a letter couched in curious stilted terms of honorific syllables, thanking his loyal friends of Kyoto for the cakes and other presents sent along the broad Tokaido to cheer him and his fellows in their days of hiding and of abiding the time when they dared strike in revenge for their lord and master, when they dared strike in accordance with the highest principles of Bushido. And there are other souvenirs and memories of those heroes who are so deeply enshrined in the heart of every true son of Japan.

Ichi Riki! To many it is but a Japanese tea house and restaurant where geisha play the samisen and posture gracefully in what this nation calls a dance. But to others it is almost a shrine, it is the Ichi Riki, and to them that name means much.

The Seventh Night of the Seventh Month

TONIGHT, the seventh night of the seventh month, if the skies are clear the Princess Tanabata will cross the River of Heaven, or the Milky Way, from her place of exile on its eastern bank to greet her husband-lover. Tonight, if the skies are clear, in all those parts of Japan where the people have not forgot the tales and myths of other days and where the Way of the Gods is still preferred to the Way of the West, the family altar will face the garden while the whole family will feast under the light of the stars. Little children will compose poems, young men will make merry, young women will sing and play the samisen, and the older couples will turn their faces upward toward the Heavenly Lovers and dream of their own days of youth.
Tanabata Matsuri!

In the days before Commodore Perry knocked at the doors of the nation, the Tanabata Matsuri was one of the five great festivals of the Empire of Japan; today it is still observed where the outer world has not penetrated too deeply. In 1873, at the instigation of the embassy returned from America and Europe, the Tanabata dance of young men and young women was abolished by order of the Tokyo Government.

In the days of the Gods, runs the old, old story that comes from China but that has been garbed in Japanese dress, there lived in the sky Tanabata Hime, or the Princess of the Loom, the beautiful daughter of a heavenly god whom none could surpass in industry and modesty. All day she sat at her tanabata, at her loom, weaving steadily. At last her father took pity on her and gave her in marriage a handsome young cowherd.

From that day on the Weaving Princess forsook her loom and devoted her whole time to her husband, so that her father became very angry and banished her to the eastern shore of the River of Heaven, which we of the West call the Milky Way. Only once a year does she cross the river to greet her husband, cross it on a bridge of magpies with wing tip touching wing tip, but if it rain that night the waters of the river are so high that she can not make the journey and must wait another twelve months. For that reason young lovers often compose their poems about the Weaving Princess, and the diaries of the Court ladies of Old Japan are filled with them. Lafcadio Hearn has told the story as only he tells such a tale.

This morning, in the rural districts of Japan where the matsuri will be kept with all its old-time ritual, the children will go out at sunrise to gather drops of dew from large leaves and use them for mixing the black ink with which they write their poems. But they need paper for this, so the rest of the day they will cut brightly colored paper into proper shapes for little Japanese poems.

A large branch of bamboo is used as decoration,

and between its green leaves are tied the poems which have been written by the children and older members of the family. The white and pink and purple poems flutter among the green leaves of the bamboo branches, while on a specially constructed altar are offered fruits and sweet dumplings to the Heavenly Lovers.

The seventh night of the seventh month is to-night, since Japan has adopted the Gregorian calendar, and on this night the Tanabata Matsuri, or the Festival of the Stars, or the Festival of the Princess of the Loom, or the Wife's Festival, is observed, but when the seventh month was kept according to the lunar calendar of Old Japan, which would make it early in the month that is now called August or perhaps, some moor month years, even in September, the children hea d the story of the Weaving Princess and her cowhere ' lover, the young men and the young women dreamed their dreams of the future, the old men and the old women turned their faces upward, dreaming of the past, and, if the skies were clear, the star that the West calls Vega and the East calls Tanabata Hime really crossed the River of Heaven and was on the western shore of the Milky Way for one night with her cowherd lover.

This Morning

THIS morning a soft April rain is falling and I look across the little lake through the opened shoji. It is bathing the delicate pink petals of the cherry blossoms, refreshing the tender green that is budding from the drooping branches of the willow tree, cutting through the sharper foliage of the gnarled pines that half-hide the dark, unpainted board walls of the houses opposite. On the roof of one of these houses is a flimsy platform built for drying clothes.

It is only a clothes drying platform this morning, but last night it was more. The soft gray rain fills the garden, clings to the cherry, the willow and the pine before it strikes the surface of the lake there to dance its fairy dance. Last night the garden was flooded with moonlight and the fragrance wafted from a distant flower, a fragrance as heavenly sweet as that of the magnolia—and with music.

In the season when the cherries bloom, say the Japanese, man does not govern his own actions but is borne along by the spirit of the blossoms just as the petals themselves float through the air when stirred by the breeze. And so, singing and strumming a banjo-ukulele, we passed out through the opened shoji and down into the garden and around the tiny path that encircles the tiny lake with its bulrushes and its golden carp and its myraid pollywogs of Spring and one lone, ancient turtle. The moonlight sifted through the blossoms of the cherry trees above us, and the needles of the pine.

There on the platform that is built on the roof were our neighbors. Two or three students, an older man, the little maid servants of the household, all were gathered there in the bower of cherry blossoms, listening to the melody and smiling. A patter of hands and low laughter, followed by a call for more, and we in turn laughed back.

The ukulele was hushed as we climbed the ladder of bamboo, mounting through the flower-laden branches to the platform on the roof. The eerie light of the full moon fell on the faces of the students and the maids, softening them into vague dimness like the faces of sweet flowers in an evening mist. The blossoms and the spirit of the blossoms were round about us, and for an hour or so we laughed and sang and drifted beyond the rigidity with which life on this earth is conducted. There were no differences of tongue for this short space of time, no differences of race, religion, pigment of the skin. The flowers and the moonlight and the music made of this little spot a world apart, governed by its own gentle laws and usages.

This morning a soft April rain is falling and I look across the little lake through the opened shoji at a flimsy platform built for drying clothes. It is only a clothes drying platform this morning.

May Day

FROM out the mists of the gray morning that ushered in the month of May the roofs of the white watchtowers that guard the palace-home of the Emperor winged their way upward from the inner moat. Nearer at hand, sprawling over much space, stood the temporary barrack-headquarters of the Metropolitan Police Board. Its black-coated servants, some with gold shoulder-straps, formed a solid barrier of human flesh and law across the wide entrance of the palace grounds. Ten feet apart, lining both sides of the broad street, they stretched toward Sannodai and toward Ueno Park.

Throaty and deep-toned, so dull as scarcely to be song, rose the roar of the slow-moving line of laborers on parade. Tall banners bearing workmen's mottoes and smaller banners of gay colors, of red and purple; green, yellow, blue and gold, waved above the seven thousand sons of toil as they paced the distance from one meeting place to the other on this May Day. Police were in the forefront and were scattered all the way through the long procession. Each little group was headed by another band of those black clad combatants of "dangerous thoughts."

It was so simple. There was no desire to strike down the powers that be. There was no need of thus closely guarding the men and women who work and labor in the factories that Japan may live. There was no danger that these seven thousand would overthrow the Empire which they love and honor with a patriotism as intense as that of the police themselves.

And it was so futile. The police were earning their pay; that is all that labor asks in turn, to work and to be compensated and to let others work as well.

The "danger" that lurks in "dangerous thoughts" can not live without food, and it is police, the drastic repression by the authorities, their futile fear of labor, that provides this sustenance to the enemy which they so dread.

The Immigration Law

THE delicate pink petals of the blossoms of the cherry trees in the garden of the Ministry of Foreign Affairs in Tokyo were fluttering to the ground that afternoon in mid-April short years ago. One or two drifted through the open window to fall gently on the thread-bare green rug covering the painted office floor of the Foreign Minister as he sat behind his desk, facing a little group of American newspaper correspondents. Last spring, and the spring before that and for many preceding springs as the world blossomed with joy each April the garden of the Ministry had been transformed into a fairyland of lacey beauty by the pink of the blossoming trees above and the green of the lawn below. Today some of those famous old cherry trees are gone; where once was a broad expanse of greenness carpenters noisily erect ugly wooden barracks because the brick walls of the main building which crumbled from the earth shocks of Japan are gone; the beauty of the blossoms is still glimpsed here and there, floating above the unpainted, weathered timber like pale clouds of pink mist.

The office used by Japan's Minister of Foreign Affairs is a large room, bare save for the faded green rug, a half-dozen leather chairs with sofa to match, a ship's washstand, a screen before the doorway and a flat desk behind which Baron Matsui sat. There is a map on the wall.

The Minister had invited the correspondents of American newspapers and news agencies to call on him that afternoon that he might talk to them of the passage by the American Senate of the clause the purport of which is to bar Japanese entrants to the United States by means of legislation, to talk of the blow which Japan had received from a nation long its friend. The six of us who responded and the American advisor to Baron Matsui sat quietly waiting while he glanced through the typed statement, prepared in advance, which he wished to make. He raised his finely modelled head, smiled his welcome and handed out the statement.

There was something pathetic in that statement, something pathetic and noble in it and in the situation. The Foreign Minister of a great Power was appealing through the press to the people of another nation that justice might be done his countrymen. It was a tribute to the power of the press, but equally a tribute to Japan's abiding faith in the sense of justice and humanity of the American people.
"There is not much that I can say in complying with various requests for an interview. But this I do want to do: I want to appeal against the final passage of the proposal designed to exclude Japanese * * *." The statement went on, couched in terms of politeness but breathing the seriousness of Japan's deep wound, went on to tell of how Japan had recently been affected by America's desire to curtail armaments and by America's unquestioning response to Japan's needs

when the Great Earthquake struck, went on to the closing paragraph:

"If now we get from you an experience of a different character, it will undo some of the spirit of friendship and esteem in which we have long been happy to regard you. It can not do more than this; but, with a nation the character of yours, the regard of others is, we believe, a consideration of no mean importance."

We finished reading the formal statement and then Baron Matsui in well modulated tones began to talk to us, to tell us of how Japan felt regarding America's action, of how nothing but the good impulses and ideals of the American people could avail in this present crisis, of how we, as the link between the American public and Japan, had a duty and a privilege as great as his own. "My task," he said, "is to establish and maintain good relations through governmental channels; yours, to further them through a fair understanding."

In that bare room, filled with the sunshine of a late April afternoon and with an occasional drifting cherry petal, with the Minister of Foreign Affairs seated at his desk, there passed swiftly the changing pictures of the recent years, the picture of the Japan of a few years before filled with ambition not always worthy, of the Japan proud in its own conceit and believing itself independent of all other nations, of the Japan that lay stricken and suffering in the torrid heat of a September noon of earthquake, of the Japan that set bravely to work to rebuild what Nature had destroyed, of the Japan that went into the money markets of the world and paid a heavy price for the gold it needed, of the Japan of that afternoon, humbled and contrite, conscious that no nation is sufficient unto itself alone but must live in charity and mutual helpfulness with all the countries of the world and which, so it seemed, was being refused that charity and helpfulness by the nation which of all others it had been taught to believe the most altruistic, the least self-centered, the most impartial and just.

The sun drooped lower in the west. A single, tiny promise of pale pink fragrance floated through the window and settled softly on a corner of the Minister's desk.

We left the room to go to our task.

Service Completed

THERE is happiness and rejoicing today throughout the length and breadth of the Eight Great Isles of Japan. In thousands and thousands of homes elder sons and young sons are being welcomed back after having served with the Colors for nearly two years. Bugles are blowing and banners are flying in the streets of Tokyo, of every city, village and hamlet of the Empire.

Nearly two years ago, one bleak morning in January, these same lads were marching through the streets also, but then their faces were set away from their homes and towards the barnlike barracks that house the soldiers of Japan. Banners were flying then, too, and bugles were blowing, but the atmosphere was entirely different. It was an atmosphere of courage and of willingness to serve the Emperor, but there was none of that overflowing happiness, that bubbling joy with which Japan is pervaded today.

There had been farewells the night before, and the neighbors had gathered to bid good cheer to the youths who had been chosen from among their fellows to wear the khaki uniform of Japan for two years. Neighbors formed little bands which marched from the home to the barracks, and at the head walked those who were being inducted into the army. At the gates of the barracks that crown the hills of Tokyo, that dot the shores of Tokyo Bay and that are scattered here and there throughout the Empire, farewells were said, and the youth of the nation entered upon its period of service with the Colors.

Not every boy in Japan who reaches military age is chosen for the army. With a standing force of less than two hundred thousand, this is not necessary. Eliminations had taken place, first by physical examination, then by exemption of those necessary for family support or enrolled as students in some college or university, and finally by the drawing of lots, for there were still more conscripts than the army needed. Only one out of every potential seven is required, and only one from every seven is taken.

They were congratulated, those who were to enter the army, and they accepted the congratulations. And yet, probably not one of every hundred but envied his fellows who had been exempted. He was ready to serve, since the Emperor needed him, but he would vastly have preferred to remain in civilian life. Scarce a lad in the Empire today really desires to serve with the Colors but scarce one rebels if he be chosen.

The two years that have passed since today's rejoicers marched from their homes to the barracks have been long ones for them.

This morning, before the dawn had fairly broken, the streets of the cities and the villages of Japan were filled with marching neighbors and parents, all headed for the military posts. Revile sounded, and the men to be discharged sprang from their cots where most of them had lain the night through, talking and gossiping, too excited for sleep. The last exercises were gone through and the last army breakfast eaten, and then the gates leading to the barracks were thrown open. Through them streamed fathers and mothers bearing civilian clothing for their sons. Eager, excited, happy greetings were exchanged, and in a few minutes uniform had been doffed for kimono or for coat and trousers.

One by one the discharged lads stepped forth from the military compound into the street; and cheering Banzais greeted each of them. Friends and neighbors joined with parents in forming little cavalcades as they took up the march through the streets back to the home of the returned son.

Feasting and rejoicing are the order of the day, and happiness reigns throughout the whole of the Empire.

Japan in Manchuria

HE turned to run, dodging behind a crowd of chattering, laughing Japanese in that town of Mid-Manchuria; and so I had to close my unused camera.

He could not have been more than twelve years old, this blue-coated boy of China. Like all his fellow-countrymen, he labored. He had come with curious eyes to stare at the gaiety of the festival that the alien islanders, far from home, were holding in this Shinto shrine on his natal soil in honor of their Great Sun Goddess. The grounds looked new and barren. It is easy to transport the body, but the soul of a people seems indigenous to the soil and does not move rapidly about on railway trains or in the van of pioneers.

He was a boy, and the bright booths, the gaudy toys, the laughter and the music brought an answering smile to his young lips as he stood there in the blistering sunshine, shifting from foot to foot and jiggling the little burden on his back. The child was fretful. The heavy holiday kimono was too warm. From time to time the boy of China turned his head, bringing his face close to that of the Japanese baby strapped to his shoulders, and whispered a word or two in Chinese or with broken accents in the child's own tongue.

I stood watching them, this strangely sorted pair, watching and dreaming, and wondering what his haughty forbears, those who once believed themselves to be the Lords of all the East, of all the world, might think. The boy seemed happy. But I wondered.

And then, slowly and cautiously, I drew my camera from its case. I wished to keep this living, breathing picture of the meeting of Japan and China. The smile faded from the eyes of the boy and there came another look. He turned to run, and, with a sigh, but not for the lost picture, which I keep in memory, I closed my camera.

Foreboding

THERE is a rambling old inn on the outskirts of Tokyo, not far from the home of the Prince of Satsuma, with a garden of quite marvellous rocks and winding pathways and a little lake overlooked by the tea houses of the inn and by two old cherry trees that were planted by Iyemitsu, one of the greatest of the Tokugawa Shoguns. Iyemitsu, my host tells me, was fond of journeying to this spot to hunt with his falcons. Iyemitsu is to me a living being, for if one refuse to become acquainted with the ghosts and spirits of the Japanese who have gone before and who still hover about the places they love and who still influence thought from which grows action, then indeed one will never know the half of Japan.

Iyemitsu, thinker and administrator of his day and age now three centuries gone, may be here in spirit, but there is another group of men of this century who are present in the body this evening just before the winter has broken into springtime. They have wandered through the garden and have enjoyed its quiet peacefullnes, and now they are seated on clean mats of one of the semi-detached tea houses and are partaking of an excellent Japanese dinner.

They are eating, but the food is the smallest and most insignificant part of the feast. It is the words and thoughts in which they are absorbed, for they are examining critically and scientifically the Japan of the present, and are peering anxiously forward in an endeavour to envisage the Japan of the future. The host, a brilliant man, possesses the pessimistic outlook for his country's future which is common to nearly all intelligent Japanese since the Great Earthquake, and he sees gloom ahead. An overcrowded Empire without a sufficient food supply and without an outlet for emigrants; a people who lack the skill and efficiency of the West in industry and trade; a land with no great natural resources other than water power and copper; a nation that has grown to greatness by military and naval power and that finds that power now to be sadly out of joint with the times—what does Japan have that gives promise of the future? He examines the nation piece by piece, dissecting it dispassionately, and comes to the conclusion that there is no factor which gives cause for optimism.

And I, the foreigner, agree with all he says—except his conclusion. He has left out one factor, and that the most fundamental. "If," I ask him, "we were back sixty years and attempting to predict Japan's future, and we had made the prophecy that has actually come true, had asserted that Japan was to become one of the foremost Powers of the world, we would have been laughed to scorn, would we not? And yet Japan was poorer then than now, and the struggle for existence among the nations was just as intense. What brought Japan to her present high place? One thing only: The character of the Japanese people, some force within themselves, for you have eliminated all else. That is not gone, and you have no right to discard it in predicting Japan's future. You say that that spirit was one of militarism, and that the day of militarism has passed. The spirit was not militarism; militarism was the harness which it wore because that was what the times seemed to demand. That harness is out of date now, and useless. The new harness, the harness of this economic age, has to be put on the Japanese spirit and character, and I for one believe Japan will learn to wear it as efficiently as ever she wore sword and rifle."

The Internationale

FROM seven throats there rose in its Japanese version the words and stirring notes of the "Internationale." Two bars, two bars and a half, and then one of them more cautious than the others stifled his companions, knowing the dire penalty in Japan of thus giving voice to "dangerous thoughts."

It was only for a moment, for from another table in this ultra-Westernized cafe of Tokyo two new voices caught up in echo the refrain, and carried it forward another bar or so.

Six bass voices and one shrill treble of the earlier group joined in, and for a few minutes the walls resounded with the condemned song; but no aftermath ensued.

It was a curious performance, now bold and daring as the voices swelled unto the roof and were flung back from the four walls, now slow and cautious, dying almost to a whisper as their better judgment gained control.

The two in the corner, unable to hold their own with the larger group, broke into shrill whistling that must have carried to the nearest of the ever-present police, and still farther. But no interruption came from the law.

They wore beards, ridiculous half-grown but much encouraged beards—six of that group of seven. The seventh was a lad to whom the razor must still have been unknown. He was that pathetic type of youth whom the police of Japan gather in their widespread net and trumpet forth that thus they save the Empire from Communism.

The song rose and ebbed, keeping time and giving index to their wavering courage. It was beer, of course, beer, sake and strong whisky that gave the temporary courage to these half-baked proletariats.

They were in a place for beer, and for vastly more dangerous thoughts than any catalogued by the police of Japan. That was their protection.

This curious cafe, supposed to be a reproduction of New York or Paris, paid its heavy tribute to the law, and so gained the desired protection. The protection was for an ugly business; not for incipient Bolsheviks. But the protection was all-inclusive, and so, for an hour or more, these two groups of semi-rebels broke forth in the forbidden song, vented their discontent in a way that brought them relief and happiness and that did no harm. It did more; this evening's triumph would suffice for many, many "dangerous thoughts." The police, unwittingly, had done far more toward curing social discontent than if all nine had been arrested, tried and sent to prison, and so forever confirmed in their resentment to the existing order.

Azalea

THE most brilliant flower of all the Empire is breaking into its riot of glorious gorgeousness that pricks into brilliance the green and misty isles of Japan. On the slopes of mountains and along the banks of rivers, in parks, in temple courtyards and in many, many private gardens the red and scarlet and crimson, the magenta and the tawny pink, the white, the purple and the heliotrope of the azalea have begun to flame.

The cherry blossoms have faded and the petals of the virgin plum were scattered long ago. The sword blades of the iris are just beginning to guard their lovely blossoms of deep purple or of glistening white, and the delicacy of the wisteria is trembling into fragrant life. The resplendence of the peony is yet to come, but the glory of the azaleas is already claiming tribute.

No aristocrat of flowers is the azalea, but a commoner whose home is everywhere. No quarter from its prouder rival blossoms does it ask, but blithely wages its own battle to make this world more lovely.

Scarlet and crimson and red, heliotrope and magenta, a tawny pink, a golden yellow and a chalk-like white, these and the colors of an over-brilliant rainbow are the weapons wielded by this blossom of the lowlands and the mountains, in the courtier's garden and the public park.

Roof-trees

THE summer lilies and the more delicately tinted blossoms of the iris crown with a line of brilliant color embedded in its own green foliage the roof-trees of the thatched huts of the peasants of Japan. The rains of late May and the warm sunshine of early June have caused their buds to unfold, and through all the terraced mountains and the narrow coastal plains of the Dragon Fly Islands these roof-tree blossoms now are awaying in the breezes of the season.

It is the sword-like blades of the iris leafs that the peasants want atop their roofs to guard against all evil and to wage valliant battle for the dwellers whom they shelter.

The thick, shaggy roofs of thatch with low, projecting eaves are a drab monotone of colorlessness all through the fall and winter. It is only when the springtime comes that along the wide ridge poles tiny shoots of green appear. As April comes and passes and on through the month of May these green leaves stretch closer and closer toward the sun they love, and as the summer breaks each year the roof-tree irises burst into colored bloom.

Whether the evil spirits fear the sharp-edged leaves or not, certain it is that these stately blossoms crowning the low roofs of peasant huts wake happy spirits in the hearts of passers-by.

Snow

SNOW, that white purity of mysterious beauty, had fallen and the ground had frozen and all was well with the Hakone, the chain of mountain grandeur which gives birth to earthquake and volcano and which pays the penalty of all motherhood—the agony of pain and the decay and desolation that follows birth.

That was last night, and this morning was—this morning.

The sun broke from its filmy bonds of gray clouds, and the matchless glory of Fujisan stood out sharp and distinct. The glistening peak reared proudly above the shoulders of lower lying mountains that have sought to hem it in. The scars of the Great Earthquake lay concealed beneath the beauty of the snow. The branches of trees drooped toward the ground beneath their weight of purity. The golden sunbeams danced over all, and man was glad that he lived, glad from the sheer glory of brute life, glad from the wondrous ecstasy of loveliness that the brute can never know.

The Heralds of Spring

THE hand-bells of pilgrims with the skirts of their long kimono tucked up to reveal white underclothing have ceased to echo on the air of Japan in welcoming the Higan, the great Buddhist Festival of the Dead that marks the vernal equinox, and Spring is once more provoking these isles of misty mountains into a rebirth of beauty.

The Heralds of the Spring are to be seen and heard about the dusty streets of the cities and in the greener country-side, while the soft veil of rain that now and again wraps everything in its life-giving embrace has a moisty warmth that has been lacking for many months. The trill of a nightingale or the chirruping of some tamer bird floats across the bamboo fence enclosing a little garden where the peach and plum are in the full glory of their blossoming. Perhaps a passing breeze catches up a few stray petals of pure white or brilliant pink to carry them over the man-made barrier and toss them gently against the cheeks of those who move through the narrow, twisting lanes on this hillside in the heart of Tokyo.

The Heralds of Spring—the birds, the flowers, the breeze, the rain and the young of humankind—are proclaiming the coming of their beloved season.

Like the glimpse of a flowering tree in the midst

of a snowstorm a vendor of gold fish comes down the street. Across his shoulder is a long swaying pole, from which depends a basket at each end filled with tiny bowls of tiny gold fish. He walks with the peculiar swinging rhythm of the coolie-bearer of Japan lest he disturb his burden. The movement is all from the waist downward, and his shoulders glide steadily through the air, the pendant baskets swaying with the gentlest of rhythms at the ends of the long pole. The vendor of gold fish in Japan is the first of the Heralds of Spring, and the dwellers in the cities gladly heed his call.

The tinkling of many little bells, of bells of glass and bells of metal and bells decorated with long grasses and bright purple streamers, is heard, for the wind-bell is the chorus of man's music that greets the Spring. The street merchant with this load of harmony pauses while a bride purchases two little bells of glass which she will hang in some corner out of doors that is swept by the breezes from the south and west, there to tinkle merrily and tell the tale of joy that the Spring brings.

And there comes a hand-cart with its buckets of ice cream and shaven ice colored a bright magenta or pale saffron by fruit juices. Truly the Spring is here when the ice cream vendors begin to displace the sellers of hot sweet potatoes. The sturdy bare legs of 'rikisha men, shorne of their tight-fitting cloth trousers of the wintertime, pad through the streets in response to the season. At night the Ginza is crowded by the throngs of strollers out for a breath of April's air. Every flower store is filled to overflowing with great jars of sweet peas and other blossoms of the early months. Plants and trees and seeds are offered and are bought on every hand.

The first of the country cousins are beginning to make their way from their inland homes to the wonders of the capital. From thatched huts that stand in the midst of low-lying rice fields and from tiny homes that cling perilously to some mountain precipice they come up each year to behold the glories and the marvels of Tokyo. The ground has been prepared for the trans-plantation of the tender green shoots of young rice and the rest of the work on the patchwork farm put in shape so that for a few days they may be absent from their homes. And so they come up to the capital!

What marvels indeed does Tokyo present to the mountaineers from rural Japan who have long saved and scraped for this life-crowning trip! The 'rikisha pullers, too, are in the height of their glory, for they act as guides, walking slowly from place to place, pointing out the sights and dwelling on them in a way that would be the envy of conductors of the sight-seeing busses of the West.

The Imperial Palace grounds must, of course, be visited, and the country men and women pause before the gates across the moat, there to clap their hands thrice and bow in reverence to the home of the August Mikado. Kudan Hill, where all the spirits of New Japan's soldier-dead are enshrined, attracts. Temples and shrines and spots that have figured in the history of Japan are visited, but these are not the true marvels.

It is the inroads of the West that bring the deepest

wonderment, the visible mechanism and material creations of modern civilization. All must ride upon the subway. The tall buildings of brick and stone and steel and concrete, one of them full nine storeys high, the others six and seven and eight, are to these peasants of Japan more wonderful than are the tree-embowered shrines of their own past. The Marunouchi Building, christened the Marubil by the Japanese, the largest building in all Eastern Asia, holds them spellbound. Within its vast confines that reach upward seven flights are housed more people than their own village holds. Truly it is a wondrous thing. The Marubil, work of an American building firm, has made a deep imprint upon Japan. There is a Marubil soap and a Marubil hat, a Marubil this and a Marubil that, for the name is one to conjure with and the merchants and manufacturers have not been slow to make good use of it.

There is much room for thought and speculation in this fact. Is Fujiyama yielding place to such a pile of steel and concrete as the Marubil for the symbol of Japan?

A Japanese Cape Cod

IT is so difficult for the Westerner living in the port cities or the capital of Japan to form a picture of this Empire that embraces the broad foundations upon which the present and the past Japan is built. The towering, ugly buildings that have been so plentifully sprinkled among the tiny wooden houses of a day gone by tell the tale of the inroads made by material Western civilization in the Far East, but their frank commercialism sounds no note of the innate courtesy, the leisurely and perfected workmanship, the artistry and the ideals of loyalty and honor bred into every Japanese. The buildings represent not his heritage from his ancestors, the very basis of his life and existence, but, rather, what he has acquired and added to that basis, the flaunting but less substantial superstructure of modern Japanese life.

It was with delight, therefore, that we took the little train which, leaving Tokyo behind, rounded the head of Tokyo Bay, cut eastward across the neck of the Boshu peninsula and puffed to a halt at the station of Choshi, where innumerable jinrikisha and one of the three motor cars of that town of forty thousand citizens were drawn up to serve the passengers coming from the capital.

On the trip around the head of the bay we had

for traveling companions in the second class coach an army officer, his wife and children, evidently bent on a week-end outing; another family of some half-dozen members or more returning to a little village on the peninsula for a visit with the grandsire of the group; a miscellaneous collection of individuals, most of them showing plainly that they were sons of the soil or of the sea, although one or two wore the fancied finery of the West rather than the more graceful kimono and sandals of Japan.

The spring had broken a few days before, and here and there the white of a plum tree in full bloom or the crude pink of peach blossoms stood out from the background of scraggy pines, of the delicate tracery of bamboo foliage and of low hills covered to the top with wild grass or terraced upward with rice paddies. An occasional field of rape added a brilliant yellow to the scene that was predominatly green.

All along the route, as the train paused for a few minutes at each station, we had been the objects of curiosity. The "Honorable Barbarians from the West" were quite evidently a novelty in this section of the province, only a few hours from the city of Tokyo but isolated from its surging tide of progress. That we were still near the capital of Japan was evidenced only by the presence of many, many soldiers, for the land around the head of Tokyo Bay is dotted with post after post, barrack after barrack, filled with the soldiers of Japan in their uniforms of khaki and great, uncouth shoes which must be a sore trial to feet accustomed to the freedom of toe-sandals of straw or wood.

The curiosity was not one whit diminished at Choshi itself. Not only the school children who had come down to the station to while away the closing hours of daylight, but their elders as well stared at us with eyes wide open but containing no trace of animosity, merely the simple curiosity of the children themselves. It was a fete day in the town, and the queer strains that come from a Japanese band attempting to play Western music rose from the vicinity of the Buddhist temple that was nucleus for the celebration. A motion picture house, showing films of American manufacture, stood in the temple enclosure, and was the chief attraction of this rural Asakusa Park.

Through the town and on out toward the ocean we went, to the Japanese inn that is called the Gyo Kei Kan and that overlooks the broad Pacific from the point of land that, of Japan proper, stretches fartherest toward America. It is an inn that is known to Japanese throughout the Empire, but the foreigner seldom touches there. The shoji and amado are of glass on the side that looks out to the sea. Below them the surf crashes and roars against a rock-strewn beach and breaks into spray over giant boulders that jut into the air above the water a few hundred feet out. To the left, the point curves even farther out into the Pacific, where it is crowned by a tall lighthouse of white stone, built more than a half-century ago, the pride of the neighborhood, the emblem which figures on all Choshi products from the labels on the bottles of excellent soy sauce to the bath towels that the Japanese inn presents to each departing guest.

At night the long beam of light from the tower sweeps across the restless sea that lies bathed in moonlight or tossed by storm; at dawn the sun emerges red and glowing from its bath in the waters of the Pacific. By day and by night there is ever present the song of the surf and the whisper of the wind in the pines to landward. Peace and leisurely ease; contentment and beauty—the restless, turbulent Japan of the present has been left behind and that other Japan re-entered, that Japan of daimyo and samurai, of artist-artisan and simple farmer, of bushido and cha-no-yu.

"A sort of Japanese Cape Cod," reads the brief description of Choshi given in the guidebooks. Certainly it is a land where the sea yields a living to men. Shell fish and eels, tiny sardines and giant halibut and salmon, are of far more interest to the people of Choshi than are quotations on the stock exchange or the wages paid for day labor. There are farmers, too, and there is one little community which finds a livelihood by moulding and baking clay into the gray tiles that roof the nation's homes. The old men and the women make and mend the nets; the young men put out to sea in ponderous boats with square-shaped sails when the weather is fair.

All along the beach that sunny Sunday morning there were picnickers. They had come, bringing lunch, and playthings for the children, to sit in the warmth of the spring sunshine and gaze out over the waters. Some climbed the hundred steps to the lighthouse and beheld its wonders. Little shops that dealt in tea and cooling drinks and curios, mostly made of shell, were doing a good business.

Farther up the beach, around a second point, there lay a fishing hamlet. At each end a rope of rice straw, remembrance and tribute to the Great Sun Goddess of the Shinto Faith, had been stretched between two saplings and formed a simple arch across the road. The torii, the sure sign of a Shinto shrine, dotted many of the hillsides, as did graves the beach. Curiously enough, the one great Buddhist temple where the fair was held seemed to be the only evidence of that religion in this bit of old Japan.

The Kimigayo

IT was on a steamer, an ocean liner, ploughing westward through the waters of Balboa's ocean to reach the East that we heard it first. It was on a Japanese steamer. For three nights we had our American motion pictures and for three nights more we had our American dances, most decidedly American dances. And for the seventh night we had that most un-American of all American things—the moonlit witchery that drifts through the wavering palm leaves fringing the shores of the magic isle of Oahu.

But, a few nights later, we heard it! On the second or third or fourth night after the routine of dances and of Douglas Fairbanks and Mary Pickford and all their coterie, we had a glimpse of the land toward which we were moving.

It was a Japanese vessel. The crew and the cabin boys stripped the uncouth alien clothes from their lithe limbs and quickly breathing chests. A ring of soft rice-straw rope was thrown down on the upper deck, and the circle was strewn with whitened sand. Four sloping poles, one wrapped with black for the South, one with white for the West, one with green for the East and the fourth with the scarlet, that denotes the North, supported a purple canopy on which was emblazoned the tre-foil crest of the Tokugawa.

The lights glimmered on sweat-covered legs and arms as we in evening dress, in turn, formed an outer circle of human beings for—we knew not what. It was for the happy joy of Japanese amateurs playing that they wore the belts of the giant wrestlers of Ryogoku, the idols of sport-loving Tokyo.

It was not that night, but it could not have been many nights later, that we heard it. August thirty-first was the day that we should have thrown overboard as we crossed the dateline sailing westward into the East, but—it was a Japanese vessel. In late October we were to gather in the garden of one of the palaces of the capital to honor the official birthday of the Emperor Taisho, but August thirty-first is his true natal day, and what captain of a Japanese vessel would disregard that fact?

In the morning we had met in the dining salon to toast His Imperial Majesty in champagne, but I had been late in arriving and so had not heard it then. The whole day was a holiday, a holiday at sea, but still I did not hear it. Not until that night, under the rays of the full moon of matured summer and sailing on a southern ocean did the strains of the "Kimigayo" reach my ears.

They tell me it was German who composed it, who composed this national anthem of Japan. If so, it is a tribute to German greatness of soul. For there is nothing else which so nearly approaches in sound an expression of the true Japan. There are English translations of the words—but what do they matter!

Japan, with her Jimmu Tenno and her Eight Great Islands and her Emperor Meiji, owes a debt, an unpayable debt, to that German who listened to the heart-beat of a nation and put it into notes and measures that the rest of the world, too, might listen.

The City

FROM the hilltops of old Tokyo dull gray roofs of tile or deadened, post-earthquake tin stretch in every direction as far as the eye can reach. Here and there a patch of green tree-tops stands out vividly like an island of welcome color in this dry sea of monotone. Buildings, the sharp-edged structures of stone and brick that men use for offices, just upward like the fingers of some cubist model. Tokyo is not a city of beauty from above.

Nor is it lovely from the ground. It is merely an enormous background of neutral tinted grayness.

Etched against this sober dullness, with all the quick eagerness of the color-prints of Hiroshige or of Hokusai, is seen a little child in brilliant hued kimono, green branches of a drooping pine bent down to kiss blue water, a glimpse of Fujiyama through a bower of cherry blossoms or the graceful lines of the severely simple torii of the Shinto Faith.

Throughout the Day

ACROSS the bridge of stone, hewn by the loyal hands of the youth of Japan in honor, tribute to their great Emperor Meiji, swept the car, swerving sharply first to left and then to right to emerge upon the dusty, wide parade grounds of Yoyogi.

Near at hand, stretching flat across the broad plateau, the barren field of many, many acres was covered on this crisp November morning with the swift-moving figures of Japan at play. Servant lads and students, apprentices from the shops, the sons of middleclass families housed in tiny homes with tinier gardens had sought the open spaces of Yoyogi this Sunday for their recreation.

A cloud of dust as some amateur enthusiast slid to first base as he had seen it done in pictures spurted into the air. The forecasting shadow of the New Year tide could be perceived in two little girls playing battledore and shuttlecock with the past season's playthings.

"Ball one!" "Strike two!"—the words of English from these throats of Young Japan, clad in kimono or proud baseball uniform of cotton, rose shrill above the other sounds. Truly the national pastime of America has made conquest of these Isles of Sunrise.

Nearby and spreading wide in all directions, this vast plateau in a most sadly overcrowded city of four, five, six, near seven millions, offered space and dusty air to the young generation of Japan. The Commons of Tokyo, whether they be Hibiya Park, Yoyogi or some other spot, are always, ever filled with boys, young men, who escape so easily from humdrum.

Then the eyes lifted. Out beyond the spreading field where the plateau drops into a fringe of trees, there in the open sky floated the fairy vision of perfection—O Yama!

Ethereal, mistily nebulous, the pure white of the glory-cone of Fujiyama seemed a half-substantial filament of wondrous gauze in the cloudless but still dust-bedimmed sky. Adoration through the centuries, the adoration of a people for the beautiful, was understandable. What need of creed or dogma, priest or church or even the belief in the Princess Who Makes the Flowers to Blossom? O Yama fills the heart and spirit with that unattainable completeness sought by man, sought and some times, for a brief space of time, achieved.

All day the August Mountain hovered as a protecting spirit of pure beauty over the flat plain of Musashino. Through the "neck of the bottle," weaving in and out among the conglomerate, ugly, distasteful traffic that throngs the narrow roads leading from the city, there prevailed the soothing consciousness of the mountain's nearness. Unpainted houses, the more hideous gewgaws of post-earthquake architecture called hyogen, hid His August Loveliness now, but the presence was felt, even in the midst of drab sordiness.

The heavy traffic left behind, the car roared over the well trod gravel road into the open countryside. Now a clump of leafy, lace-like, feathery bamboo filled all the world, and then O Yama took its rightful place of triumph. The car would plunge into a tunnel of deep pines, into the flaming glory of the autumn maples, the grayness of a village street, but always, always, ever and again there would come the open spaces of the rice and mulberry clad moor, and then, floating in the ether, the beauteous grandeur, majesty, sheer loveliness of the mountain.

Across the rock-strewn bed of the turbulent Tamagawa with its flimsy makeshift bridge the Mountain of Perfection held forth its promise as does a rainbow when it settles somewhere midst the shacks of cities.

Across the sere fields that had already yielded rice and wine this year, across the patches of dwarfed mulberry, across onions, evil-smelling daikon, even worse, there waved beckoningly the mirage of the Peerless One that is not a mirage but which, if one be wise, one keeps in that charmed state and refuses even once to tread with boots its slopes.

On and on the motor purred and roared. Nearer and nearer, yet knowing that the goal would not be reached, plunged the car.

Into the prosperous town of Hachioji and out again to enter a lovely valley winding upward to the pass with its clear gurgling mountain stream growing ever louder, more insistent, more a part of life, the drive continued. Past the holiday throng that climbs Takao San and into the green gorge beyond it rushed the car. Up, up and up—across the tiny crest, and then the mountains in hushed silence dropped sheer away.

A valley lay below; uneven hills and mountains clad in green and in the flames of autumn rose on the yonder side; beyond, higher, nearer Heaven, floated in the misty sky the white glory of the Sacred Mountain.

What We Call Progress

THE opaque paper screens that form the windows of Japan were pushed far back in their silent grooves, leaving a wide open space above the low window sill through which there streamed the moonlight of late March. Spring, with all its magic witchery, was in the air that night. The petals of the plum had fallen with a slow-silent fluttering, and the branches of the cherry trees had not as yet been touched into that filmy cloud of beauty in which all Japan floats as in dawn-colored mists with the coming of the month of April.

In the Eastern Capital, a scant three hours away, snow lay on the ground and a cold wind swirled and snarled about the gray, sodden streets and the sharp-edged buildings that Japan has chosen to adopt from out the Western World.

Here in Atami, sheltered from the east, the west, the north by friendly mountains that stoop down to kiss the foam-flecked waves of that beloved Sagami Bay, the warmth of spring touched all with its caress.

Since the days before men knew how to record history on paper, little Atami has nestled thus in the shelter of the high Hakone Mountains that rim it round on all sides save the south and so shelter it through the winter season. The feudal chieftains who fought back and forth over the narrow coastal plain and the mountain passes of Japan for control of the Empire passed by this warm nook. Within short distance of political Kamakura and later of political Yedo, the inaccessibility of Atami insured the village a peace that few spots in the land then knew. Only by creeping along a narrow ledge of cliffs that broke sharp from their summits to the very sea itself or by arduous clambering over high mountains could Atami be reached, for the Japanese of other days were far from a seafaring people despite their island home.

Peace came under the Tokugawa Shogunate, and later there sailed to Japan from out the West an American Commodore, whose advent worked the greatest revolution that the land has ever known, a revolution far transcending any fought with arms. The battles that surged back and forth across Japan were no longer those by knights in armor but consisted of the struggles between an ancient civilization and what we choose to call modern progress. A victory for the invader was marked by the building of a huge factory, the creation of another bank.

Still Atami led its smiling, leisurely life amid the flowers and the oranges that the warm southern sunshine brought with the New Year and that blossomed on through the next December. The customs that had endured for centuries still lived on. Isolated by its hills and by the sea, the little village with its multitude of hot springs and its marvellously beautiful coast line remained a bit of Old Japan while so much of the Empire slowly changed its ancient garb for one of modern industrial civilization.

This is to vanish, and Atami is rejoicing. Engineers, trained in their science in America and Europe, have tunneled through the cliffs, have bridged the chasms, have extended the railway the short eighteen miles along the mountainous coast which so long served as a wall against the outer world. In time, the heart of the Hakone Mountains will have been cut through by a tunnel more than five miles long, and then Atami will be but one little station on the main line between Tokyo and Kobe; will be a way station on the path of modern progress.

If Atami realizes and appreciates this, still Atami rejoices in the future, and is holding a celebration for the coming of the railway. This celebration is a matsuri, a festival of Old Japan, such as their fathers' fathers held at times of rejoicing.

The moonlight bathed the blossom-decked town in an ethereal brilliance. Its wide path of brightness stretched across the waters, broken here and there into a rippling stream of silver as some stronger, more courageous, more insistent wave rose above its brothers to reflect the light as it broke into a plumy crest of foam. A dark headland rearing skyward pointed the promontory to the right, and to the left the curving bay shore lay in graceful scallops, one upon the other, mile after mile, even unto that long stretch of coast that is Miura and that could be seen faintly, wanly, nebulously yet real, through the softly brilliant light. A tiny light gleamed and danced on the water far away as it moved slowly onward to be engulfed at last as the boat which bore it passed between the low headlands that give entrance to Tokyo Bay. Far out to sea the feathery spiral of smoke that forever ascends from the volcanic cone of Oshima rose into the night air.

Behind the pine-fringed shore lay the village, pricked into being by the many, many lights in its homes and inns and along the lantern-lined streets. Great clouds of milky steam, painted with a gold or silver sheen as they caught the lanterns' glow, rose from the hot springs, and it seemed that the laughter and the music of the happy villagers floated like a more lovely cloud over all.

The throbbing of a drum rose on the air, for Atami was celebrating with a matsuri the coming of the railroad to the town.

Hope for the future, hope of gain and progress, was the message brought by these two long lines of steel that now stretch from this bit of Old Japan until they link with other rails and steamship lines that sail to all the world. Hope for the future; death to the past—this was their message, but if Atami heard and knew it, still the town rejoiced.

The winding, tortuous streets, at places paved with great slabs of stone, fit only for the foot or for palanquins and a terror to a motor car, are soon to go. Thatched roof and driftwood fence will yield to steel and concrete structures that are the temples to that modern god—Efficiency. Even kimono and the light-tapping wooden geta must give way to coat and trousers, skirt and blouse and leather shoes, for the "spirit of the times" is stronger, more efficient even more insistent, than the Spirit of the Past, and its triumph is assured if once it gain a foothold such as is now given by the railway.

That is for the future. Tonight, this bit of Old

Japan, unknowing, or, if so, not caring, of the fate that lies before it is rejoicing in its own defeat, rejoicing in the manner that its fathers and its fathers' fathers joyed in at the festivals of the myriad gods of Shinto and the adopted deities of India, then China, then Korea, that took on the color of their alien island home.

Three mummers, one dressed as Daikoku Sama, the god of wealth; one as Sukeroku, idol of two conturies of theatregoers; one as a nondescript figure from out the Past, burst into the little tea-house by the shore, frolicsome, exhuberant, filled with the spirit of the evening yet quite self-possessed.

One grabs the drum sticks of the maiko and makes resound the stirring rhythm of the "Lion Dance of Echigo." It swells in a great chorus till the breaking waves themselves are vanquished. The rhythm is contagious, and the plaintive words of the old folk song come from the throats of those gathered about the glowing coals of the hibachi.

Suddenly, without a note of warning, the drumming stops, and the erstwhile drummer shouts to his companions, to Daikoku Sama and Sukeroku, that they must be off, that other places, other guests and other friends are waiting for the coming of these mummers to make glad this night of gladness.

On one of the lower hills of the coastal town, just where it corners so that the whole sweep of the broad bay is visible, stands the town hall. On its matted floor are seated half Atami's semi-plutocrats, the men and women who earn the plaudits of their fellow-townsmen because of their munificence.

On the simple stage, draped in the five colors of

the theatre of Japan, which rises above the mats across one end of the long room sit the amateur musicians. This is their night of triumph, and no enjoyment could be more complete than theirs as one strums a samisen, one blows into a shakuhachi, two strike with dignity their drums and the voice of the fifth rises in the wailing falsetto that is music in this land.

Two lads, scarce in their teens, and an older, strapping youth dance to the strains of this music. They are dressed in red and blue and yellow, black and white. This is a time of festival, and not of overnice appreciation. Fisher-lads, perhaps, by day, or workers of some other sort; but tonight they are the links between this world of fact and the more pleasant world of fantasy. Their dance is strenuous; success is theirs; the seated figures leave the every-day behind and float on the wings of loved imagination into that dream-world that so few will ever know, for those who have it know it not and strive ever after something else, something which they so foolishly believe finer.

This is a matsuri, a great festival, that the ancient, ancient happy town which nestles underneath the mountains, close by an ever-balmy southern sea, smiling and content through all the centuries, is celebrating for the coming of the railway that will link it with the modern world of industry, machinery and remorseless competition that is known to all of us.

Gardens

THERE is scarce a house in all Japan that does not possess its garden. Many a home has not more than two feet square of ground, but in that small compass there will be found growing tiny dwarfed trees, a curiously shaped rock or two in good proportion to them and perhaps a lake a few inches across. The whole is a unit, and so perfectly done that the miniature dimensions fade from mind as one gazes at it, and it seems the dusty city has been left behind and the wide countryside entered.

In the house that does not possess even so small a bit of soil as this, still a garden will be found. In such a home it is contained in a tray of rough earthenware, usually quite flat and rectangular or oval in shape. The proportions are even smaller, but the scene is there and the same impression of the beauty of Nature is obtained.

The home of the rich man has its garden, too, but it is one of many acres. It is more magnificent and diversified, but it is not one whit more satisfying than is the diminutive garden of his neighbor-workman.

The Japanese house is simple; the Japanese garden is simple also but it is ritualistically simple. "One should spend at least as much on the garden as the house" runs a Japanese saying, and it is a saying practiced by many.

It is in the garden, more than in the house that happiness is to be found.

Ghosts of Kamakura

THERE was little light from the half-moon and from all the stars. It was enough to touch the three golden chrysanthemums into phosphorescent life, to awaken them to gleam in ghostly splendor against the darkness of the ridge pole of the Buddhist gate that spans the path of stone leading to the Great Buddha of the Minamoto Shoguns in the sleepy town of Kamakura.

The wind-shaped trunks of pine trees reared to right and left, their needle-foliage forming a near-solid mass through which the beams of the half-moon could find faint entrance. Behind, there glowed the lights of some cafe, but here was darkness, darkness impenetrable and substantial save for the dim outlines of the massive gate and the other-worldly glimmer of the sixteen golden petals that symbolize the Goddess of the Sun and of her earthly children, and whose keeping is in the hands of His Imperial Majesty.

Through the gate and up the stone-paved path we went, beneath the thickly clustered pines and their black shadows. There were no pilgrims now, no throngs of sightseers. How can the meditative Buddha love the worship of the chattering, geta-clattering millions who disturb thought and peace of soul by the triple clap of hands?

The Daibutsu in the sunlight with the wavering

dance of water-reflected sunbeams on his breast is one thing. The Daibutsu in the moonlight is another. And still another is the Daibutsu veiled in rain or in the mists of green and gray Japan. This was the Daibutsu, calm, silent, loving, living underneath the stars and the pale silver of a half-born moon.

Shadows, the shadows of this world but soft and clinging, claimed the giant image for their own. The light touched the face and here and there the seated figure, glinting dully on the weathered bronze. Peace and eternal calm and happy, quiet content spoke from the lips that seemed just trembling into audible sound. Life, but a life enduring, lifted far above the petty and the mean, was in the lines of the arms and throat as they emerged from out the molten darkness. Majesty, serenity, compassion—a living, wise and loving friend was sitting there in the opaque summer night.

There rose a chorus from the frogs which find their home in the ponds and pools of the surrounding gardens. From somewhere in the sleeping village came the clink of a night watchman as he made his rounds, planting his kanabo firmly with each step that its jangling metal rings might tell all that all was well. The distant bark of a dog and the fretful wail of a small child were borne by a slight breeze through the night. The sounds but added to the silence, pricked it out in semi-detail as the moon-beams filtering through the needles of the pines disclosed the darkness.

We turned, this time to face the Buddhist gateway with its heavy, sloping roof and guardian demons. The open square was filled with golden light, the light of street lamps and of windows. Silhouetted in the foreground by this glow there sloped the trunk and branches of a seaside pine like unto the pines that grace the wood block prints of Hokusai, Hiroshige. What artist of an earlier day obeyed his instinct so to plant that pine?

Out beyond the gate there lay the sea which never sleeps but which, like the great Daibutsu, speaks of peace and calm and of eternity, the one through motion and the other through the quiet repose of stillness.

The waves were breaking on the deserted beach, rolling in one upon the other with the ceaselessness that knows no change. The vibrant, whispering ocean breathed slowly and dispassionately. Dark purple, almost midnight blue, its immensity was streaked with dancing silver as the waves broke in long undulating lines to cast themselves upon the beach. The wan moonlight and the pale flicker of the stars so far above dropped down to kiss the surf and touch its darkness into light.

Seven centuries ago the waves broke thus; seven centuries ago the Daibutsu sat in calm serenity. Seven centuries ago the warriors and the ladies of Old Japan moved and had their being, lived and loved and died, beneath this moon and on this beach, worshipped and prayed to the Daibutsu. The Minamoto and their followers, the Hojo and their clansmen, the men and women who directed the course of Empire were here in presence. Are they gone?

The ghosts of Kamakura slumber through the heavy, drowsy noon and throughout the waking hours. In the moonlight and the starlight, in the mists and in the shadows, they return in rustling dresses, they return in clanging armour, and they walk the beach at midnight, kneel in worship to Daibutsu, live and love and have their being in the places that their lives knew, form the dreams for us poor mortals, let us know they are not mortal.

The Most Sacred Rite

THE shrill wailing of Shinto music, the slow tread of the religious processional and the crackling of watch-fires alone broke the deep silence as the Sacred Mirror, emblem on this earth of the Great Sun Goddess, was solemnly and reverently borne from the simple shrine in which it had rested for the past two decades into the adjacent new shrine where it will remain for another twenty years.

The flickering of the firelight and the torches cast gigantic shadows against the dark cryptomeria of the forest in which the shrines rest at peace. The garments of the priests, white and of many colors; the bows and arrows and other ancient weapons; the long wavering silken walls in motion that enclosed the bearers of the object which above all others is most sacred to millions upon millions of people burned themselves into the brains and hearts of those watching the rite so deeply that they became a permanent memory.

As at the time of the Enthronement ceremonies, when the Kashiko-dokoro is taken from the Imperial Palace in Tokyo to Kyoto and then brought back, here was the very soul of a nation laid bare. It was impossible to see the rite so sacred to Japanese and remain untouched.

Save for the Enthronement ceremonies of the Emperor, there is no other rite in all Japan which approaches the Shikinen Sengusai, the transfer of the Sacred Mirror to its new shrine, for stirring the hearts and soul of the Empire. As on the night of the Daijo-sai, silent prayers are raised in a multitude of homes throughout the islands.

The mirror, gift of the Divine Ancestress to the Heavenly Grandson whom she charged with the subduing of this earth, is regarded by all orthodox Shinto believers as representative of the Sun Goddess herself. It is, to them, the most sacred object existent.

The one discordant note in the solemn processional which was held after the sun had gone down and while the rains were falling was the presence in it of high dignitaries of the Court, of the Premier and other officials of the Government in the gold braid and black knee breeches of modern court costume.

Throughout the day the Premier and others had been received with acclaim as they moved through the little town of Ise, site of this most sacred shrine. The village was filled with thousands of pilgrims, yet the customary sleepy atmosphere prevailed. Streets were bedecked with flags and lanterns, and handsome torii covered with pine branches had been erected in front of the railway station. All day long devout visitors thronged the grounds of both shrines, offering prayers. Contrary to the usual custom, most of these worshippers knelt on the ground when making their devotions. Elderly people, particularly women, most of whom probably never expected to see rites again, predominated.

The new shrine for the Sacred Mirror stands side by side with the old, forming a striking contrast which is provocative of thought. One is ancient and weather beaten and extremely artistic; the other is blatantly new with gleaming white wood and glittering decorations. All of the branch shrines in Ise had also been re-constructed. Sakaki branches and other Shinto emblems were everywhere.

There is no more sacred spot in all Japan—and so, to the Japanese, in all the world—than this shrine to the Sun Goddess in Ise. Within the innermost sanctuary of the simple wooden building of primitive architecture rests the Sacred Mirror, wrapped in pure silk and cased in an unpainted box of white hinoki. Of the Three Sacred Treasures, the Mirror, the Sword and the Jewels, which constitute the Imperial regalia of the realm and are the tangible symbols of sovereignty, the Mirror comes first.

Back in the days of the Gods, before the creation of this lower world, runs the orthodox Shinto version which is taught in all the schools and which all Japanese are expected to accept on faith, the brother of Amaterasu Omikami, the Sun Goddess, angered his divine sister and she retired into a cave and the world was cast into darkness. Distressed and perplexed, the other Gods and Goddesses devised a scheme for enticing her out. Drums were beaten, a young Goddess danced on an upturned tub and a mirror was flashed into the cave.

Amaterasu Omikami, wondering that others could be happy without her presence and hearing that one more beautiful than she was outside, ventured forth, whereupon a great stone was rolled before the mouth of the cave that she might not re-enter it. She was handed the mirror and, gazing into it, saw reflected the beauty of her own features.

Later, when the Sun Goddess dispatched her Heavenly Grandson to conquer and subdue these islands of the earth, she handed him the Three Sacred Treasures, admonishing him as regards the Mirror:

"Whenever you gaze upon this, the Sacred Mirror, you behold our sacred selves reflected in it. So regarding it, you will find it holy, and must therefore reverently worship it, keeping it beside your couch and in the privacy of your chamber."

The Mirror was in turn delivered to Jimmu Tenno, the first earthly Emperor and founder of the Imperial line, and from him has passed into the keeping of Emperor after Emperor, down to his present Imperial Majesty, one hundred twenty-fourth in lineage.

Nearly an hundred years before the birth of Christ the Emperor Suijin caused replicas to be made of the Three Sacred Treasures, and the original Mirror was sent to Kasanui that it might not be exposed to the gaze of the vulgar, the Emperor keeping the replica with him in his palace.

In the year five A.D. the then Emperor, Suinin Tenno, again removed the Mirror, this time to the banks of the river Isuzu, the present Ise, where a shrine was built and its care entrusted to an Imperial Princess, Yamato-hime-no-Mikoto. It has remained there since.

In time of peril or in time of great joy, in sorrow or in victory, an Imperial Messenger has been dispatched to the shrine to inform the spirit of the Sun Goddess of the events then transpiring. When an heir to the Throne was born or an Emperor died, when a new Emperor acceded to sovereignty, when the capital was moved or the palace rebuilt, when danger threatened the nation and when the enemy had been defeated was such an Imperial Messenger sent.

The Emperor Meiji went twice in person to worship at the shrine, and the present Emperor has gone three times: On his departure for Europe, on his return and immediately following his Enthronement ceremonies at Kyoto.

Shinto, with the hatred of that which is soiled and of pollution, decrees that each twenty years the Sacred Mirror must be removed into new shrine buildings. The removal is conducted with ancient rites known as the Shikinen Sengusai.

The new shrine is an exact replica of the old, and that of the one before and of others for many, many centuries. It is credited with being pure Shinto architecture, with being a replica of the primaeval Japanese house of worship, but here and there are notes which denote a more recent influence, such as the brass decorations and the screen before the entrance gateway, which is curiously reminiscent of the spirit screen of China.

It stands in a great park of one hundred sixty-four acres at the foot of Mount Asama in Yamada. Bridges and torii give entrance to the park and are scattered along the graveled pathway which leads to the inner shrine, the Kodai-jingu, the Naigu. Trophies of Japan's two modern wars stand grimly in the outer grounds of the shrine. The path sweeps along until it touches the banks of the Isuzugawa, the clear waters of which run with a softly murmuring song over a pebbly bed. At this point pilgrims stop to droop down by the bank of the stream to cleanse and purify themselves before going farther.

Turning from the stream, a forest of giant cryptomeria is entered, the tall stately trunks of the trees and the sombre green of the foliage making of the out-of-doors a temple in truth, creating an atmosphere in which it seems that the Gods of the archaic past well might choose to dwell. No sound is heard save the crunch of the geta on gravel, the organ-chorus of the wind among high branches and the cries of birds.

The shrine structures are of the simplest. A high wall of unpainted wood surrounds the rectangular compound within which they stand, and before the entrance is a screen of the same material. The small building containing the Sacred Mirror is in ancient Shinto style, the roof beams projecting to form an X, the ridge pole extending at each end, the structure raised above the ground on posts and a narrow verandah encircling it. It is made of hinoki wood and thatched with the bark of the same tree. It is like the Yuki-den and the Suki-den wherein the Emperor performs the rites of the Daijo-sai at the time of the Enthronement.

The front is open but is hung with curtains of purest white silk which flutter in the breeze. Within rests the Mirror in its silken wrappings and its box of plain wood, the Mirror upon which no human eye has gazed these many centuries and which is the most sacred object in all Japan.

To the right and left and slightly to the rear stand two lesser shrines, one dedicated to the spirit of the God who drew the Sun Goddess from her cave and one to her own grand-daughter. There are nine branch shrines in Ise. The Outer Shrine, dedicated to the

Goddess of Cereals and Silk, is in another part of the city.

The old shrine is brown and weather beaten; the new is of glistening white wood. They stand side by side, and each twenty years the Mirror is transferred to a new shrine, when the old one is torn down and cut into tiny slips of wood to be sold to the millions of pilgrims who visit there during the ensuing double decade.

The erection of a new shrine for the spirit of the Great Sun Goddess is not a simple matter. Eight years before its time of dedication Shinto ritualists and workmen gather in the forest high on Mount Kiso and hold a ceremony in honor of Misoyama, the deity protecting the trees there. Felling of them follows, and the work proceeds, twenty-six ritualistic ceremonies in all being conducted, the crowning one of which is the Shikinen Sengusai. There is a ceremony when the logs are floated down the river, and again when the first log is sawn, and again when construction actually begins, and there is a ceremony for the god of earth.

The workmen taking part belong to families who have held this right for generations. They are purified each day, lead austere lives and are garbed in white as they go about their labor. A soiled garment, or even a spot of blood, calls for a special purification.

The Shikinen Sengusai, the culmination of these eight years of preparation, is held but once in twenty years; it has survived for more than two thousand. It is essentially primitive, although accretions have been gathered with the passing ages. It is the primitive expression of a primitive religion which is more than a religion, which is the basis of a unique society and upon which has been reared the political structure of a State able proudly to take its place in the forefront of the modern nations of the world.

It is difficult, if not impossible, to separate the religious, the political and the patriotic in Japan. The three are closely interwoven. The respect and reverance accorded to this symbol of Amaterasu Omikami is not due to religious faith alone. The position of the Imperial House, guardians of the treasure, must be taken into account.

And so, to those few, especially to those three from an alien land, who witnessed the Shikinen Sengu-sai as the gentle rain descended it seemed indeed as if the heart of Japan were laid bare.

The procession itself was a colorful scene of beauty touched with mysticism. The ancient style robes of the priests and the ritualists, the archers and the sword-bearers all blended into a picture which seemed more picture than reality. Reed instruments wailed in plaintive music and the flickering light which played over them added to this sense of illusion. The setting of the shrines with the forest as background lent an air of awe and of the sense of primitive man. Only the modern Court uniforms were an anachronism.

Slowly, so very, very slowly, with a restraint that was dignity itself, the procession of figures from another and an earlier age emerged from the weathered shrine and descended the rude stone-banked terraces that served as steps. The sacred emblem was enclosed within four long walls of silk that wavered along the path, propelled by unseen bearers. With time-obliterating footsteps the processional passed beneath the giant trees, unconscious of the respect and worship of the honored few who witnessed it, turned to right and then to right once more and bore the Mirror into the building of gleaming new wood which is to house it for the next twenty years. The time consumed was not long when measured by a clock, and yet it was in reality the whole life of the Empire of Japan.

From a reading of the Kojiki and the Nihongi we of the present day may get at least a glimpse of that Japan of the past which has almost vanished but which still lives on. In many countries a nation's or a people's past lives only in the printed word and in the heart; in Japan institutions and ceremonies that antedate written history still survive. The Shikinen Sengusai is one such.

The rites of the transferrence of the symbolical representation of the spirit of the Divine Ancestress of the Yamato Race to its new home have been conducted again and yet again throughout the centuries. At times, as the worldly fortunes of the Imperial Court waned, or as the mind of the people was turned from religio-political matters to warfare or some other distraction, the rites have suffered. But always they prevailed and, sooner or later, have been restored to that high place to which they were originally destined by a mystic people to whom the Gods are ever close.

With the restoration of full earthly power to the hands of the young Emperor Meiji more than sixty years ago there came about a revival of the Shinto faith with the Emperor and his Heavenly Ancestors as the center. Some of the foreign scholars of those days called it the invention of a new religion. It was not an invention; it was a revived survival.

The ceremonies and the underlying significance of the Shikinen Sengusai are such a survival. They fit in perfectly with the revival of Shinto and give it justification.

Million upon million of Japanese have trampled the roads throughout the centuries which lead to the Ise Dai-jingu. This was true before the days of the Tokugawa Shogunate, but it was especially emphasized during that long period of rest from civil warfare. The young apprentice of what was then Yedo believed that, unless he made the O Mairi, the Great Pilgrimage, no future lay before him. As a result, the Tokaido was filled with youthful aspirants to this or that trade, impudently begging their way from door to door until they reached the shrine of the Great Sun Goddess and there did obeisance.

In these modern days of easy travel by railway many a Japanese keeps postponing the day of his O Mairi, since it can be so easily done. But no statesman is appointed to high office, no unexpectedly great fortune is received, no overwhelming disaster takes place but that the one affected should perform this ancient obligation. What was done two thousand years and more ago is still done today.

Japan is changing, changing so rapidly that it is difficult to keep pace with the movement. The sleepy village with its willow tree lined streets that was Tokyo scarce a decade ago has given way to a great city with scores of buildings of steel and concrete, with well paved streets, with automobiles instead of 'rikisha, with up-to-date department stores, with cafes and bright lights and jazz and mobos and mogas. What is in progress in Tokyo is indicative of what is in progress, in greater or less degree, throughout the country.

The visitor, even the foreign resident, may look at all this and say: "Here is the real Japan." The more romantically inclined may go into the less frequented towns and cities where life still moves somewhat as it did in the days before the Emperor Meiji and say: "Here is the real Japan."

Both are right; and yet each is but partially right. The "real Japan" is composed of both these phases of life, and underlying them both—these two extremes—running strong and steadily as it has throughout the ages is found the dayspring of Japanese being.

Tonight at Ise the upper surface was stripped back and the all-pervading current of a nation's, of a people's strength was revealed to that little group which watched the procession bearing the Sacred Mirror from its old home to its new.

The present was forgot; the past seemed not to exist. For a brief space of time there seemed to be no time. It seemed that once more the Gods who made Japan and who still watch over it walked the earth.

There are great waves of emotional reaction in any people which well up and well up until the crest is reached. Recent years have afforded two such crests to the people of Japan. One crest came with the passing of the Kashiko-dokoro to Kyoto for the Enthronement ceremonies of the Emperor; the other with the rites of the Shikinen Sengusai at Ise.

The Seal of Japan

CHOSEN Jingu, the State Shrine for Korea of the Japanese Shinto cult of Emperor, hero and ancestor worship, has been consecrated to the service of the Great Sun Goddess, of the Emperor Meiji and of the Empire of Japan with simple, symbolical rites. The Emperor was represented at Seoul by a special messenger; Korea was represented by Prince Yi Yang of the Korean nobility; the political state of Japan was represented by the Tokyo-appointed Governor General of the dependency.

Korea has been "adopted into" Japan by this ceremony far more than it was when the political annexation took place, so far as the thought life of the Japanese people goes. What the mental attitude of the Korean people may be is another question and is one to which I can not find the answer.

There stands arching over the road that leads out of Seoul to the distant capital of China a great gateway of pure white stone. In years gone by it was called the Tribute Gate, for beneath it passed the messengers of the King of Korea who were sent each year bearing tribute and gifts from the vassal Kingdom to the Son of Heaven who sat upon the Dragon Throne in his moated palace in Peking. When the yoke of China was thrown off the jubilant Koreans re-christened their gateway that leads toward China, calling it the Arch of Independence. When, so short a time later, the Korean State was extinguished by the Empire of Japan, the newcomers from the Sunrise Isles sought again to change the gateway's name, but wiser councils prevailed and it was not done. Instead, the Chosen Jingu has been built and dedicated.

Seoul is a city that charms and entrances. It lies sketched on a plain bordered by mountains that come down to the city's edge and wall it in, leaving a great gap for entrance at but one spot. It was the tip of the crest of one of these mountains, of that called Nanzan in Japanese and Namsan in Korean and South Mountain in English, that was chosen as the site for the shrine that is Japan's most visible and perhaps most tangible symbol of conquest. Nanzan stretches out into the city as does a peninsula into the sea, and it is at the very tip that the shrine is built.

The Shinto cult is a simple cult, having but little ritual and almost no theology. It is one of the few pure Japanese products dependent not upon the influence of China. The Government in Tokyo has decreed that it is not a religion, that it is no more than a cult of patriotism, and all Japanese must be Shintoists, be they Buddhists, Christians, Koreans or what else besides. It is, in essence, ancestor worship, although the Japanese Government prefers that the word "reverence" be used. Its greatest God is Amaterasu Omikami, the Great Sun Goddess, who is the ancestress of the Imperial family. There are other gods, eight myriad of them, among whom are all the heroes and great men of Japan. The Emperor Meiji, who brought

Japan from seclusion to its place as a great world Power, is not the least among them. The Great Sun Goddess and Meiji Tenno were chosen for enshrinement in the Chosen Jingu.

The Emperor of Japan was pleased to present a sword to the shrine. The sword, together with the mitamashiro, which means "representatives of the soul," that were to be enshrined were taken from Japan to Korea by Viscount Sonoike, the Imperial Messenger. In the late afternoon his train drew into the magnificent new railway station at Seoul, the first train to enter it. Tact and diplomacy prevailed, for the first to welcome the mitamashiro was Prince Yi Yang, acting on behalf of his deposed Korean Royal Family. The Japanese Governor General, other officials and the foreign consular corps came next.

A palanquin of immaculate, unpainted wood, borne by specially selected Korean youths clad in white, was carried forward to receive the mitamashiro, which, covered with a fine cloth of green silk, were placed therein by Shinto priests and Court officials. The sword that is the gift of the Emperor, sheathed in a scabbard of plain wood, was laid on the palanquin, and all were borne to their temporary resting place in front of the great torii that leads up four hundred steps to the shrine. There they were placed in chests and carried up the long flight of stone to the Hall of the Imperial Messenger, to await the shrine's dedication three days later. The glow of the setting sun struck the white and golden green and jet black of Shinto robes and head-dresses, lacquered footwear, as the trumpets of the military guard of honor rang out across the city below celebrating with fire-works and merriment.

Three days later the dedication took place. At ten in the morning the mitamashiro were borne into the inner shrine, the Imperial Message was read and offerings presented. Prince Yi Yang of Korea, purified by the waving of sakaki branches before him, stepped forward to make an offering of tamagushi. He was followed by each in turn. Profound silence was relieved and accentuated by the footfalls of the Imperial Messenger as he passed up and down the steps of stone in his black lacquered shoes; reed flutes shrilled and wailed the music of prehistoric Japan in which Shinto found its birth; the modern trumpets of the military guard of honor beyond the second torii seemed a distant sound.

There were no gorgeous decorations, a few halberds, shields and streamers of five colors alone being used. Long rows of offerings flanked the inner gates, the gifts of the Imperial Family, the Korean nobility, the officials of the colony and others throughout the peninsula.

Thus did Japan set the seal of its national soul upon Korea, even as it had set the seal of its political body nearly two decades before.

The Emperor

JUST as the dark of night began to shade into the gray of dawn, to be followed in turn by the glory of the sunrise across the waters of Tokyo Bay, the highest Shinto priests and Court ritualists in the Empire of Japan gathered before the Kashiko-dokoro, the Place of Awe, within the precincts of the Chiyoda Palace, home of the Emperor in Tokyo.

The Place of Awe is holy to all Japanese, for within it is kept the ancient replica of the Sacred Mirror handed down from the Great Sun Goddess to the Heavenly Grandson, then to the first earthly Emperor and in turn to each of his successors, the Mirror that is the tangible symbol of sovereignty in Japan. A new Emperor, the one hundred and twenty-fourth of his line, which is "coeval with Heaven and Earth," according to orthodox Shinto belief, is formally to ascend the Throne of his ancestors, to make public announcement thereof and to commune with the gods of the Shinto pantheon, to eat and drink sacramental food and wine with them.

The strains of the "Kimigayo" rose on the clear air of the November morning as the gates of the palace swung wide. Across the inner bridge moved the Imperial cortege as it began its progress to the ancient capital of Kyoto. Across one bridge and then doubling back across the second that is parallel and lower it wound, and out into the great park that fronts the moated castle-palace.

At its head, borne on the shoulders of sixteen stalwart lads from the little village of Yase who were garbed in ancient costume, moved the Feather Carriage, a square palanquin draped in rich brocades and encasing the Sacred Mirror.

The early morning sunlight lay aslant the palace park and touched into glory the Ark that bore the Mirror, that bore the very soul of the Japanese race. The colored garments of the Youths of Yase, moving forward with a curious shuffling stride just as their ancestors had moved for generation upon generation when they had performed this service, gleamed against the white gravel of the roadway and the gray stone walls of the palace arising from green banks that touched the waters of the moat and were crowned with winged watch towers of pure white. The standards of the Emperor and of his Empress followed the Sacred Mirror, and the crimson pennons of Lancers of the Imperial Bodyguard fluttered in the gentle breeze of dawn. Their Majesties and their chief retainers formed the colorful processional that came in the train of the Sacred Mirror, but the emblem of the Great Sun Goddess took precedence; the earthly Emperor came second.

The Niju-bashi, the gateway and the double bridge that give entrance to the Chiyoda Palace, formed a wondrous setting for this pagentry that found its beginnings in the days before men read and wrote and that comes down to the present moment as Hirohito sets forth upon his pilgrimage to old Kyoto, there to proclaim to the world of men and of the gods that he has ascended the Throne of the Empire of Japan by the oldest Court ritual this world still observes.

All that day the train which bore the Kashiko-dokoro and the Emperor passed through the countryside of Japan, journeying on rails along the old Tokaido that has echoed to the tread of million upon million of sandal-shod feet throughout the centuries. Great throngs greeted its passage, for once only in the lifetime of any Emperor are the masses of Japan given opportunity to worship the Kashiko-dokoro and the Sacred Mirror as they make their progress through the country.

That night, before the sun had set upon it, the Mirror was enshrined at Nagoya, and the journey to Kyoto completed the following day.

Long before noon on that second day of the Gotai-ten, of the Enthronement Ceremonies of the Emperor of Japan, the broad gravelled drive that leads from the outer gate of the palace park in Kyoto to the Kenrei-mon was lined by those Japanese and a scant half-dozen foreigners who had been honored by a place along its sides to witness the arrival of the Kashiko-dokoro and the Emperor. Mists, the mists of Japan, that changed into soft rain and back again to mists, wrapped in dampness the waiting throng in their ceremonial kimono, uniforms or high silk hats and formal dress of the Western World.

The Kenrei-mon, the gate giving entrance to the courtyard in which stands the great Throne Hall, was thrown open. The gravelled drive stretched from it straight as an arrow flight through the palace park and out into the city where it became a long avenue of pavement lined with modern buildings and the simpler buildings of Old Japan, leading onward to the railway station. All along this route, from palace gate to modern railway station, tens of thousands waited patiently.

As the Kashiko-dokoro passed along this avenue and through the palace grounds there arose a soft sound like the patter of the falling leaves of autumn. It was the reverent, subdued clapping of thousand upon thousand pairs of hands as devout Japanese bowed their heads in prayer to the Sacred Mirror, emblematic of the soul of Amaterasu Omikami, returning on the shoulders of the Youths of Yase to that palace which had been its home for near ten hundred years. Once more the Mirror rested in Kyoto, true Miyako, home of the Mikado, where His Majesty was to announce to men and gods that he had taken up the duties divinely enjoined upon his line before the dawn of written history.

On the fifth day after the Emperor's departure from Tokyo the new Emperor proclaimed his accession formally to the people of his nation and to the world in the ceremony called the Gosokui-rei, but ceremonial preparations to that end and to the rite of the Daijo-sai four nights later had been going on for nearly two years. These ceremonies, beginning at the death of the last Emperor, are elaborate, replete with significance in the history, the life and the religion of the Japanese people. New rice had been sown and harvested in consecrated fields and all the other rites that have come down from earliest times and have gained accretions with the passing years had been celebrated.

On the morning of the Gosokui-rei the Emperor, purified and sanctified, had announced his ascension to his Divine Ancestress before the Kashiko-dokoro. At one o'clock that afternoon he ascended the Throne to proclaim it to the world, a ceremony which those of the West are prone to look upon as the crux of the Enthronement but which, in reality, pales into insignificance beside the Daijo-sai when His Majesty communes alone with Amaterasu Omikami and the eight myriad gods on the Plain of High Heaven and partakes of a consecrated meal with them.

The Daijo-sai is pure Japanese; the Gosokui-rei is shot through with influences that have come from China. Even the architectural setting for the ceremony betrays its Chinese origin. The Shishii-den, or Throne Hall of the Imperial Palace at Kyoto, consists of one great room crowned by a curved roof. The Emperor enters from the north and faces south, a Chinese tradition. The entire front of the hall is open, a silken curtain depending a few feet from its cornice. Before it spreads a courtyard of clean sand, bare of all ornament save two guardian trees, one a cherry and the other a mandarin orange. Along the east and west sides are covered galleries. The Sun Flower Gate cuts them on the east, and the Moon Flower Gate on the west, while the Light Receiving Gate on the south faces the Throne Room, and it is just outside this that a little group of foreign correspondents has been placed.

The hall is entirely bare except for two thrones on massive diases. The Takamikura, or High August Seat, the throne of the Emperor, rests on three stages.

Eight pillars rise from the upper stage to shelter the throne with a canopy, from the crest of which soars a golden phoenix. The throne seat is "a chair of red sandal wood inlaid with mother-of-pearl—broad-seated, squarely built, four legged and substantial." The whole is elaborately lacquered and decorated. The throne of the Empress, the Curtained Throne, is to one side and is similar save that it is smaller and has less ornamentation.

The galleries around the open courtyard are filled with diplomats and with high ranking Japanese in Court dress, some ancient, appropriate and beautiful, some modern and garish. Princes and Princesses of the Blood and the highest ranking subjects stand near the Throne. Brilliant standards are raised in long rows, adding color to the scene. Three gongs and drums are at the bases of the banners, and spear standards are near them. The guards of honor, bearing bows and arrows and with swords at their sides, guard the gates.

The Master of Ceremonies raises his voice in a warning cry that the Emperor is approaching. He enters and ascends the dias, officials placing the sword and curved jewels beside him. The Empress enters. The curtains veiling the thrones are drawn back. His Majesty stands, and all present make profound obeisance. The Emperor reads his Rescript announcing his ascension of the Throne. The Premier mounts the steps of the hall, reads an address of felicitation, withdraws slightly and leads the nation in three shouts of Banzai for the Emperor, so timed that Japanese throughout the length and breadth of the Eight Great Isles raise the shout in unison.

The Daijo-sai is the climax of the Gotaiten, or the Enthronement Ceremonies of Japan. The Yuki-den and the Suki-den, two simple buildings constructed in the primitive style of Old Japan and, with their attendant buildings, enclosed by a fence of brushwood, have been erected for this purpose. After the sun has fallen His Majesty, purified and with a tranquil mind, enters these buildings to commune directly with the Gods and to partake of a sacred meal. Throughout the Empire all is hushed and modern machinery is stilled as the nation keeps the vigil with the Emperor and the Gods, the vigil in which he takes his rightful place among the hierarchy of the myriad deities of the Shinto faith, just as he has already taken his place among the sovereigns of this earth.

There are other rites, and there are feasts and banquets and many functions before the ceremonies of the Gotaiten are brought to a close, but they form an anti-climax. On the night of the Daijo-sai the souls of men and of the Gods they believe in are in touch, and the Emperor reaches his pinnacle of greatness in the hearts of his people.

It is difficult for the American or the European with his conceptions of sovereignty and of executive power to grasp the psychological attitude of the Japanese toward their Mikado. It is difficult because no parallel, no acceptable analogy, is offered in the life and thought of the Western World. If it be said that the Emperor is regarded as God, error follows, for the divine attributes of the Emperor of Japan do not correspond to the Christian concept of Godhead. Neither does the European theory of the Divine Right of Kings of past centuries apply in Japan.

An understanding of ancestor worship and of the family system as it is conceived in the Far East is essential to an understanding of Japan and more particularly of the place which the Emperor occupies in Japanese thought. According to orthodox Shinto mythology, the Imperial Family is directly descended from Amaterasu Omikami, the Great Sun Goddess, the nearest to a Supreme Being in the Shinto pantheon. All other Japanese are descendants of related gods who accompanied the Heavenly Grandson to this earth when he was commanded by Amaterasu Omikami: "The Luxuriant Land of Reed Plains is a land over which our descendants shall rule. Do thou, Imperial Grandson, go and rule over it; and the Imperial succession shall continue unbroken and prosperous, co-eternal with Heaven and Earth."

All Japanese are Shintoists, whether professing the Christian, Buddhist or some other faith, and it has been decreed that Shinto is not a religion but a patriotic cult so that this may be possible. Shinto is, in fact, a simple religion which explains the Creation and provides for the organization of Japanese society, the existing political organization of the Empire being but the latest dress worn by this continuing organization, just as the living Emperor is but the present representative of the headship not of an organized political group but of the Japanese as a people, as a race.

All Japan is a family, and the head of that great family is His Imperial Majesty. There is accorded him, by all Japan, that reverent respect which is the homage to the head of the family in a land of filial piety and ancestor worship. There is accorded him that love which is due the father in any land. There is, in addition, accorded him the pious devotion which is the right of a divinely descended being in whose veins flows the blood of the Great Sun Goddess. The Emperor of Japan is not only political sovereign of the land but he is the father of his people, their High Priest, their direct intercessory with that Heaven of which he is himself a part.

But the Emperor is more, much more than the head of a family. He is the center of the Japanese cosmos. The concept of the Emperor is the all-powerful integrating force that makes for the unbreakable unity of the Japanese as Japanese. If one conceive of the Japanese as a unit (and they so conceive of themselves, even more so than do the Hebrews), the Emperor, and the attitude toward the Emperor, constitute the divine spark which gives that unit life. The Throne is that element which gives life to the Japanese as a people, as a race, as a homogeneous unit of humanity rather than as a political nation; is its soul.

Death can remove an Emperor, but it can not destroy the Throne as the center and life-giving spark of the Japanese people as a people. Death can take the father of any family, but death alone can not destroy the family as an institution, can not destroy fatherhood.

This place of the Emperor in Japanese life goes back to the very beginnings of the Japanese people, back to a pre-written mythology which survives and functions today as adequately as in the time of its origin. George Edward Woodberry has said: "In mythology, mankind has preserved from his primitive experience of Nature, and his own part therein, all that has lasting significance."

It has been said that Indian mythology is religious, Greek mythology social, Northern mythology philosophical and Japanese mythology political. This is true if "political" be taken as the organization of society, of a people's race life, rather than of concrete institutions of governance. Japanese mythology primarily organizes the machinery of society with the Emperor at its head as all-powerful. This was done two thousand years or more ago, and has survived down to the present day. It is the basis of Japanese race-life today as in the past, and it happens to have been made the basis of the specific political organization of the Japanese Empire in modern times.

It is astounding to American and European students of history that there has been no change of dynasty in Japan since before recorded times. If those students will look at the Japanese Throne as not a political but a racial institution they will understand this.

There have been changes and modifications, there have been reversals by armed force and otherwise of the political governance of Japan, but there has been no change in the fundamental racial organization of the Japanese as a people, of which the Throne is the core. The Throne has remained above, outside of politics, has been adaptable to their fluctuations because it was not basically political itself but more fundamental, and its most remarkable historical continuity has been the integrating force that has made for the strength of the Japanese people as a people. Throughout the centuries the Imperial Family has remained on the Throne unshaken, and it has remained there not because of political manœuvres or armed strength. It has remained there because the people of Japan have regarded it as a Heavenly created institution and have held it, consciously or unconsciously, vital to the life of the Japanese as Japanese, vital to themselves as themselves, as impossible to destroy as it is impossible to destroy fatherhood. To destroy it was to destroy themselves. The supremacy of the Throne is to them, a fact of nature, a Truth. This truth has been recognized and given allegiance by Shoguns and Regents, by all the ambitious and powerful men who through the centuries have wielded actual temporal power in Japan but always under the moral aegis of the Emperor. The unshakable hold of the Throne on the Japanese people is a moral and a psychological (one is almost tempted to say an instinctive) hold.

Prince Ito, who must be credited by the student of world history as being one of the ablest statesmen whom the closing half of the nineteenth century produced, displayed his insight into Japanese psychology and history, into the peculiar and dangerous position into which Japan had been plunged with the coming of Commodore Perry, into the political and social institutions of the world in which Japan would henceforth have to live in no better way than when he drafted the constitution which the Emperor Meiji gave to his subjects. He wrote in chapter one:

> The Empire of Japan shall be reigned over and governed by a line of Emperors unbroken for ages eternal * * *

> The Emperor is sacred and inviolable.
>
> The Emperor is the head of the Empire, combining in himself the rights of sovereignty and exercising them according to the provisions of the present Constitution.

Prince Ito thus seized upon the keystone of the new political structure of the State which the times demanded.

The period of the Restoration coincided with Japan's emergence from seclusion into the world at large, which naturally brought with it all the conflicting ideas and institutions of other nations of the world from which Japan had so long been sheltered. Prince Ito and his colleagues were quick to grasp the significance of this fact and to realize that adjustment was imperative. They sought to retain the spirit and basic principles of the Japan of the past, but to let them work out through institutions which mere contact with the West forced upon Japan. To do this they sought out the life spark of the Japanese people and made it the life spark also of the political state.

The supreme emotional hold of the Throne over the Japanese heart can not be broken unless there is a fundamental revision of Japanese psychology, unless the Japanese commit suicide as a Japanese racial unit and of that there is scant likelihood. Neither bombs nor bullets, neither, communism nor democracy, no defeat at home or abroad, promises to destroy Japan's "line of Emperors unbroken for ages eternal."

Along the Coast

THE glory of Fujiyama reared above the clouds and mists to bid farewell as the boat stood out from Yokohama. Scarcely had we cleared the breakwater that gray morning before the peak of the august mountain pierced the clouds and seemed to float there in the heavens, alone and perfect. The impressive picture remained throughout the day as we sailed along, the banks of cloud now concealing the mountain and again revealing it. No Japanese artist could have seen the mountain when more beautiful. The picture Nature painted justified Japanese art better than could hundreds of lectures and written treatises.

The next afternoon we lay off Kobe, circling about and waiting for a pilot to guide us through the Inland Sea. Kobe lay stretched along the waterfront, a great modern city, while sunshine and shadow formed a moving checkerboard on the green mountains that rise almost from the water's edge.

As the heads that guard the Inland Sea came in sight, there was a stir of excitement on deck, for we were about to enter one of the most beautiful passages in the world.

Forest covered or terraced mountain-islands rose on every side as the gray vessel nosed her way among them or slipped through Japanese fishing fleets of hundreds of junks and sampans with fantastic sails spread to catch the wind. At night we anchored until dawn so that the voyage might be made by day; the fairy lights of Japan twinkled from the rocks and shore, while lanterns bobbed serenely on the scarcely breathing surface of the sea from fishing junks at anchor.

Dawn came. The ship ploughed on through sunshine and mist, passing through the narrow straits of Shimonoseki into the sunset.

Night fell, and this night the myriad lights of the O-Bon, of the Lantern Festival of Buddhist Japan, gleamed out.

Morning found us slipping into the harbor at Nagasaki, down that long mountain-bordered strip of water, past dockyard and uncompleted battle cruiser to where the temple-studded hills towered above the city which of all Japan first knew the West.

The Ueno Mausolea

NOT peace, not solemnity, not gloom, but a strange blending of these three forms the atmosphere in the cool green and dark gray of the stone-paved, stone-walled aisles that wind through the mausolea of the Tokugawa Shoguns in Ueno Park, the high plateau that lifts itself above the factories, the slums, the temples, the happiness and the living, working humanity of the northern part of Tokyo.

The attendant temple, a thing of gorgeous, almost barbaric beauty, merges into the dim quiet of the place, for the reds and blues and gold of its elaborate decorations have been softened and dulled by the dust of the ages since the spirits were enshrined there. The twilight that filters through the gray boards enclosing and protecting the brilliant exterior seems in accord with the memories and dreams of the once resplendent and all-powerful Shoguns who controlled, successfully, the destiny of their Empire. The loose boards and clean rubbish scattered about also tell the tale of a day whose sun has gone down.

Between massive gray stone walls the path winds in and out in a small maze as the tombs of the Shoguns and their wives are passed. The gray-white of memorial tablets and of high stone lanterns that are never lit seems a bit of eternity amid the straight dark pines and moss-grown ground. Buddhism, for there is naught of Shinto here, has cast its spell over the whole. Buddhism has created the place, for no other religion could have brought into being this atmosphere of sober calm, of neutral tinted eternity, of continuing life by the slowness of change despite the smouldering of decay.

"Like a Mighty Army"

THE stirring rhythm of our present-day Crusaders could not be mistaken. The throbbing of the drum and jangling of the tambourine were the same as in London or New York or Cape Town. The crowd that had gathered round was garbed in kimono and in the square-cut coat of the coolie of Japan, but the continuous pulsation told the tale of those who have found true humility, who have lost all thought of self, who truly live their lives for others, of the crusaders of this century—the Salvation Army.

A song arose, a song whose words were strange and meaningless because they were in an alien tongue but whose tune has echoed ages long in stately churches and cathedrals dimly lit by votive candles, has echoed down to this dull, dirty corner of a Tokyo street.

And then came the words of the orator-evangelist, words that rose and fell in cadenced periods, telling of the Faith that has comforted and strengthened millions to a group that knew it not. The glare of the rude street lamp high above cast the weird shadow of the speaker on the dust; behind him a pine branch swayed against the rectangular lined shoji of rice paper, its slender needles pricked into sharp relief against the yellow glow.

Again the pulsations of the drum and of the

tambourines. Through the night air of Tokyo they reached out, out and out beyond this little corner to the hills and homes that lay half drowning in the early dark.

The crusaders were on the march; their battle lay before them and they gloried in the struggle.

From the Eighth Century

LORD Tennyson, H. G. Wells and others "dip into the future" and fire the imagination with what they find there, but it is an easier, a gentler and withal a more pleasant task to slip back into the past. In this land of Japan, with its temples and tombs, its shrines and its mouldering castle ramparts, its half-conscious and half-unconscious effort to preserve and sanctify in crystallized form the civilization and culture of bygone days, the foreigner who will but take the time and make the effort to become familiar with the nation's history and heroes will find himself amply rewarded by an increased enjoyment of life in Japan. Japan's ghosts—her long-dead Emperors and the warriors and statesmen and the priests and poets who surrounded them—offer a friendship which demands nothing more than that the living friend should exert himself sufficiently to become acquainted with them. The Lady Yodogimi and Murasaki Shikibu, Sugawara Michizane and his enemies the powerful Fujiwara, all of the men and women who have lived and had their being in Yamato may be summoned at the call of the dreamer of today who knows them, and he may step back from century to century, back even to the dim and misty time when the Gods descended from the Plain of High Heaven and the Isles of Japan were formed by the dripping drops from a divine spear.

There are places and occasions when these figures of the past come unbidden to him who knows them. Surely one familiar with Japanese history can not gaze on the broken remains of the barrier at Hakone without seeing daimyo and samurai passing through this guarded gateway to the Kwanto to pay unwilling tribute to the haughty Tokugawa. The clash of arms still rings about Sekigahara where the last great battle in Japan was fought, and the Minamoto and the Hojo move about the unkempt lotus ponds that lie before the Hachiman-gu at Kamakura.

In Kyoto, this spell of the past is felt strongly, but there is the equally strong force of the living Buddhist Church. Nowhere else, perhaps, as in Nara does one so have this feeling of having turned back the pages of time, of having drifted back to a life that has vanished in large part; and nothing else in Nara so vivifies this feeling as does the Shoso-in.

Twelve centuries ago, more than half our Christian Era, the Emperor Koken presented to the temple that houses the Great Buddha, to the Todai-ji, those articles which his predecessor on the Throne, Shomu Tenno, and his consort, Kwomyo Kogo, had used in their daily life and on ceremonial occasions, together with medicines and other of their treasures. Once a year now, during the first two weeks of November, the Shoso-in in which they are stored is opened, and a few guests of the Imperial Household Ministry are permitted to see these garments and mirrors, these swords, screens, musical instruments and games that were the finest products of the culture of the mid-eighth century.

The short ride from Kyoto to Nara is itself rich with memories of the past. Buddhist temples and

Shinto shrines and the graves of Emperors dot the hills and mountains bordering the Yamashiro Plain and on into the province of Kawachi. Such names as Momoyama, Uji and Nara itself mean much in the history of this country.

The mists that seem always to enclose Kyoto with the coming of the dawn had begun to lift and were being pierced by shafts of sunlight here and there which tore through their filmy opaqueness. The well ripened rice formed a brown carpet in the foreground from which rose pine-clad mountains on both sides of the flat valley. The dried grasses of autumn waved their plumes in the breeze, and the barren trunks and branches of the scraggy trees stood out in naked blackness. The maples were but beginning to flame with the scarlet and gold which is to them their swan song, and the fields were filled with blue-garbed peasant folk harvesting their season's yield.

The peace of Nara, which is a peace distinct unto itself, brooded over the park fringed with temples and shrines, for this was not the cherry blossom season with its throngs of merry-makers who find the sake cup even more entrancing than the blown petals of the blossoms they have come to see. Even the schoolboys hailed the foreigner not with the word "Ijin San" or "Seiyojin," but lisped "Gentleman" after him as he passed.

From the half-ruined walls of a decaying temple there suddenly arose a great furore, men's voices barking at one another and the clash of swords breaking the stillness. There darted through the gateway a silk clad samurai, defending his life with good steel against a band of pursuers. In another second the camera man could be seen, calmly grinding away as he reproduced in this modern medium a bit of the life of feudal Japan.

The gardens that surround the Shoso-in are Japanese in style, and yet they have the spaciousness and sense of breadth that is found in the gardens of the Western World. In the center, reared high on posts of cypress, stands the treasure house, made of hewn logs placed one atop another at angles that give the walls the appearance of a gigantic black accordion. When the Emperor Meiji came to the Throne the Shoso-in had been neglected. The gardens had gone to seed, there were no fences, and the beggars and extremely poor crept under its raised floor at night for shelter from the rain.

It is necessary to climb twelve or fifteen feet to reach the wide verandah that surrounds the building, one of the oldest wooden structures in the world, and when the Shoso-in is not open the planks of this Japanese verandah are taken up, affording double protection against thieves. The timbers have taken on a black tone through the passing centuries. It has been necessary at times to make repairs, the latest having been in the second year of the late Emperor Meiji's reign. Prior to that no repairs had been made since the Genroku period, but the planks that had been laid as flooring in one section then seemed new in contrast to the rest of the building, despite their own two centuries of age.

Massiveness is the term most descriptive of the building itself. The pillars supporting the roof, the flooring, the logs that form the walls all seem on a scale unfamiliar to Japan and to have come from a primitive age, although the Court of the Emperor Shomu was far from primitive in many, many ways, as is revealed by the contents of the treasure house.

To describe, list or analyze those contents would require a scholar and a critic of the highest order, and would, after all, prove uninteresting save to the antiquarian and his fellow-scholars. The building is divided into three separated compartments, each with two floors and none with windows. Once or twice the treasure has been pilfered, but never to any great extent, and even time has left intact more than two-thirds of the articles placed there first so many hundred years ago.

The marvellous condition of many but not all of the articles astounds one. That lacquer, hempen cloth, paintings on silk and rice-paper should have remained through twelve hundred years in such a perfect state seems unbelievable, except that the visible testimony is present. Not only the state of preservation, but the extraordinarily high artistic merit and workmanship will come as a surprise to those in whose minds Japanese culture of the eighth century is ranked with the contemporary culture of Anglo-Saxon England under Alfred the Great, the France of Charlemagne, the Germany of whom? There is some work of an artistic nature which probably can not be equalled today.

What a treasure trove indeed is this for the archaeologist, the antiquarian, the historian. Here, not in replica and not merely in written description, are the articles that were in actual use in the Japanese Court during the second half of the eighth century. There are shelves filled with medicines in hempen bags, and there are robes that were worn by the priests of Todai-ji. There are Japanese backgammon and go boards and the counters with which these games were played, and there is another game that was played with arrows, the shafts and the vase into which they were thrown being there. In two rooms masks of wood or lacquer line the upper walls, masks that were used by the Buddhist clergy in their miracle plays known as Gigaku, for this was long before the Kamakura Bakufu had brought the No drama into existence.

The No itself seems ancient, seems a heritage out of Japan's far-distant past, and so it is, but the culture of the Nara period antedates many of those things which we of today look upon as being almost coeval with the Yamato race. What a realization of age comes when what we of the present consider Old Japan is not represented in the Shoso-in because it had not then been born or evolved!

There are lists of all the articles in the Shoso-in, lists that were written while writing was still a young art in Japan and was unknown in most of Europe, and that were deposited with the treasure then. Some of the articles have disappeared, and the gold has long since been removed. There are orders with the Imperial signature for these gold removals. K. Kubota, scholar and curator of the Nara Museum, walks around with the foreign visitor and explains in English each article or answers any question that may be asked.

The remains of the crowns of the Emperor Shomu and his consort are to be seen, but they have fallen to pieces. It has been centuries since an Emperor of

Japan wore a "crown." There are boxes of all sorts and descriptions, and here or there a modern replica has been made and placed beside the original article in order that the design may be the better seen. There are several screens, some stenciled and some having been decorated with colored cloth pasted to the design instead of having been painted, but there is one of the Goddess Kwannon which is a painting that would rank high if executed today.

The influence of China may be discerned in innumerable ways, but there are some few articles which are purely Japanese. Not only is Chinese influence observable, but there are articles which actually came from China and from far more distant places, from Rome, even, and perhaps from Egypt. There is a Korean koto and an old Japanese koto, affording an interesting study in their differences from each other and from the koto of modern days. There are biwa, shakuhachi and other musical instruments, some of which are unknown at present. There is a harp, badly fallen to pieces, which bears every evidence of Egyptian origin, and there is glassware which unquestionably had a more Western birth and journeyed thence to the fartherest East.

There is a room in which are weapons: Swords, spears, bows and arrows; but that the Nara period was a time of peace is indisputable in the face of the great preponderance of the arts of peace—and of religion. The swords are straight of blade, for it was not until the time of the Kamakura Shogunate that the Japanese sword assumed its present curve. Some few are cornered and angled in a most horrible manner so that the wound might be the larger, more death-dealing.

The vast number of metal mirrors, far more of them than of any other object unless it be the priest masks, is the most distinctively Japanese note of the collection. The backs are ornamented in many and diverse ways, with chased metal, lacquer, inlay and other methods of decoration. The artistry and workmanship on these mirrors are of the first order. One or two are broken, for several centuries ago a thief rifled the Shoso-in of some of its treasures, but their very nature betrayed him when he tried to sell them in Kyoto, and retribution followed.

The Emperor Shomu abdicated and became a priest, and it is perhaps for this reason that religion looms so large in the Shoso-in collection. May it not be, however, that it was because Buddhism loomed so large in the Nara civilization that Shomu Tenno took religious orders?

No other Japanese Emperor has outdone Shomu Tenno in his devotion to Buddhism and his service for that Faith. The Todai-ji at Nara was built by him, and the Daibutsu which it contains was enshrined at his direction. The image was "given life" when the Emperor touched its eyes with his writing brush, and that very writing brush is preserved in the Shoso-in. The land round about and many acres of rice field were bequeathed to Todai-ji by Shomu Tenno.

Many of the articles used by him after entering the Church are stored here, as are also other of the Todai-ji treasures. There are iron needles that were used for the festival of Tanabata Hime, the Weaving Princess of the Skies, and the ornamental spades used by the Throne in the ritual of an agrarian people.

As the visitor leaves the gloom of the final room and steps out once more into the November sunshine, it is not like coming back to the present, for he is still in the garden and at Nara.

Sooner or later, however, this excursion into the past must end, but its memory will remain, and he who has that memory is the richer.

The Moon of Asia

RED, blood-red, across the dark and restless waters from where I knew Korea lay there rose the curving glory of the moon of Asia. It cast a nimbus of dull radiance that paled the stars. The flattened circle on the surface of the sea grew large, and then the perfect orb of a full moon left the waves beneath and rose into the air.

Not upward only did it move, but floated through the night sky toward me. The red gave way to gold, and the frothy tips of those high waves that cradled our frail boat threw back the light.

Upward and upward to its rightful place; the gold changed into silver, and across the broken, moon-kissed waves there stretched a path of radiance.

Lost Rapture

SWEPT by the throng through the narrow, crowded gate of the shrine of Kompira, the deity whose aid is implored by the weary, waiting mothers of sons of the sea, I was carried back by the throng and the dancing lantern light and the rhythmic beat of many drums to those first days in Japan, back through the still night air of May to that wonderland of misty, mountainous, blossoming Japan encrusted in the jewel words of Lafcadio Hearn.

It was the night of May tenth, the day of the month on which the ennichi is always held in the grounds and along the streets of the shrine, which stands near the corner that men of another day christened the Gate of the Tiger, Tora-no-Mon. Month after month, when the tenth day and the tenth night had come, I had passed the shrine and the garish wayside stalls that lined the streets, but never before had I paused.

The crowd caught me in one of its sudden eddies, and as suddenly had swept me into the narrow human current that flowed through the wooden gates of the shrine compound. To right and left were gaily lighted stalls displaying even gayer waves and charms. Barkers called out in singsong tones, but how was it possible for anyone to stem that tide of human beings to buy of them? On through the narrow gates and down the stone path of the shrine grounds I was carried, the clatter of wooden geta forming a dull undertone for shrill voices, the buzzing hum of pleasure and the thump of temple drums.

Before the main shrine the crowd was dense, but it was a reverent crowd. The incessant beat of the drums was heard. Above their monotone rose the rattle of brass bells, meant to catch the ear of the deity, and the steady clink of falling coins as they were pitched outward and downward by the worshippers. The note of a heavier drum broke on the air from a street theater, and the voice of a young acolyte was heard chanting as he replaced the fast-dying tapers. Shinto priests in white and in the more brilliant robes of their Faith sold tiny bits of mochi in twisted slips of paper, and prayers and charms. Those who surged forward from the gate paused before the shrine, clapping their hands and bowing for a moment in the silent prayer of Shinto or murmuring some Buddhist formula, for to them there was no distinction between the Faith of ancient India and that of old Japan.

These were the common people. Blue and white kimono or the dark blue shirushi-hanten of the workmen were their clothes, while many wore little more than a blue cloth coat and white, close-fitting trunks, beneath which their bare, brown legs glistened in the light of lanterns or electric bulbs. Bales of offerings and piles of daikon and onions, testimony of the simple life of the worshippers, lay heaped before the shrine. The laughter of the children stilled a second as they, too, clapped tiny hands and reverently bowed fantastically clipped heads before the spirits that were gone.

Turning from the shrine, the crowd swept out into the nearby streets and tiny bits of park, where laughter and where happiness held forth. Red, red balloons with Dharuma's face in white; great heaps of cold ice cream and salt-strewn, hard-boiled eggs; dolls and books and strips of cloth were all on sale, each in a little night-side stall beneath a blazing lantern or the cruel, unkindly glare of an electric bulb. A beggar woman stood, teaching her children how to sing for alms. Poor people, 'rikisha men and laborers who work for daily hire, swept, past, but many dropped a copper in her basket of rice straw.

The crowd swelled and eddied. At times the press was great; again there came a moment of free space. The seller of mechanical toys from out the West became the center of a group, the few students there lingered near the stalls of books. The chants of sellers and of worshippers were heard. The odor of fresh fish and radishes was strong. The red and white striped bunting of Japan lent color to the dingey streets and dark pine trees.

Almost to the iron gates of the American Embassy the crowd surged on, but there I turned, retraced my steps to a quiet, tiny park, and entered it. The music of "God Save the King," remembrance of the visit of the Prince of Wales, came from some childish mouth harp. The winding walks of the quiet park were dark. Dropping into a bench, two men who showed that they knew work sat down beside me. Both had little towels, for both were going to the bath. One wore a blue kimono; the other only his dark blue coat, his sturdy legs protruding as he stretched them out and let his heels rest on the white gravel path. A minute they stopped, then rose to go, and so did I.

Back to the glare and glitter of the tinsel shops I went, but the romance now had gone. Somehow, in that still moment in the quiet, dark park, it had vanished. I saw the books and students, the balloons and the gay charms. Interesting—yes. They showed the life of a strange nation. Fascinating—yes; but as a study, not as a great lure of love. The geta and the writing brushes, the queer boxes and the dwarfed pine trees in pots, these fascinated me, but I felt their compulsion only as a student. The food, the sights, the smells and the weird noises—they were the same, but I had changed.

I hailed a passing 'rikisha, hoping thus to entice back the thrill that I had lost. It was no use. The slow ride home, past shops and sights and sounds, was interesting. They held the interest of a race which seeks to blend its culture with my own. The incongruous mixture I saw and felt; the charm of other days sank back and died.

"*Wassho! Wassho! Wassho!*"

"WASSHO!" called the young leader, raising his opened fan in the air as his naked body caught the dancing light of lanterns of colored paper.

The signal given, there rose on the air the old, old chant: "Wassho! Wassho! Wassho! Wassho! Wassho!" the same condensed word over and over again as tiny sons of Dai Nihon pushed this way and that, bearing on their shoulders a diminutive shrine in which the spirit of a Shinto deity was riding.

"Wassho! Wassho! Wassho!"—the spirit was having a brave time of it, his shrine-home rising and falling as if on the waves of the sea or being swirled about by the eddying current of a river. The childish voices rang out on the night air, intermingled with laughs of joy and happiness.

It was the matsuri, the annual festival, of the neighborhood shrine, and here in modern Tokyo it was being celebrated just as it has been celebrated through all the centuries of the past before Japan knew the automobile, the telephone, the cinematograph and all the other products of this modern age that have so changed our civilization and our methods of finding pleasure.

For the shrine festival in Japan is a time of pleasure, not of long-faced solemnity, just as the courtyards of the Buddhist temples are the children's playgrounds. Religion in Japan is intermixed with everyday life and, in spite of the gravity of original Buddhism or the extreme simplicity of the Shinto Faith, it is not a thing to be feared or to inspire awe.

Before the gate of every house hung two lanterns of red and white paper, bearing the crest of the shrine on one side and the Chinese ideographs that denoted its name on the other. Here and there in the neighborhood had been erected temporary shrines where the people could make their offerings or pause from the merriment for a moment to clap hands thrice and offer silent prayer. Volunteer watchmen and guards, dressed as were their ancestors in the past, stood alert amid the throngs of people, for fire is the ever-dreaded menace in this land of houses made of paper, straw, bamboo and plaster.

The little mikoshi, the portable shrine that these tots were carrying, was but one of many. Each division of the district under the shrine's jurisdiction would bear a mikoshi to the parent shrine itself. Some were large, ornate and heavy, and they were borne on the shoulders of stalwart men. Others were smaller, and the youths of sixteen or thereabouts shouldered them through the streets. This one was but a tiny affair indeed, and its twenty or thirty bearers ranged in age from three or four to perhaps eight or ten.

Only the leader was older. Some younger priest, or perhaps only an acolyte of the shrine, he danced along in front of the heaving mikoshi, waving his fan and calling to its little bearers. Stripped save for a redeeming band about his waist and loins, his slender figure gleamed in the reflection of the many lanterns.

The little children wore the costume of Old Japan. Holiday kimono, tucked into the belt to leave the legs free, and a Japanese towel bound tightly round the forhead, they were the counterparts of their fathers and their elder brothers.

"Wassho! Wassho! Wassho!"—through the streets they pushed up and down, back and forth, the spirit within the mikoshi supposedly directing its erratic movements. One second it would swing violently to the right, and then with equal force would careen to the left, or perhaps would swirl around and around. In the old, old days, if the spirit were displeased with any villager this displeasure was expressed by the mikoshi's crashing into that man's home. It was communal judgment, of course, but the man whose house was thus branded was as much convicted criminal in the eyes of all as any man who today is tried by a jury of his peers.

"Wakaishu! called the leader, and there came the echo from the childish throats. On through the night the cry arose, ringing through the peaceful valley. With it there came the boom of the great temple drum, the curious tinkle of the samisen, the sounds of other musical instruments of Japan. The sacred dance was being performed in the shrine grounds; a Shinto priest stood in his black gauze cap and resplendent robes at the top of the shrine steps, waving his emblem of purification over the worshippers; hawkers of toys, sweetmeats and a thousand other objects all shouted their wares.

Japan is rapidly throwing aside her Past to don

the garments of the West. In the countryside much of the old culture lingers, but in the cities it is usually defeated by the Present. But even in the cities, now and then, there comes a breath from out the days of feudalism, or the voice of the Past comes echoing through children's throats as they shout "Wassho!" and bear along the sacred mikoshi.

An Old-Fashioned Garden

THE moon rose slowly from behind the thatched roof of the tearoom opposite that was veiled from too clear a view by the tracery of flowering shrubs. The pale light sifted down into the garden to silver it with an eerie fairness and to find reflection in the little lake.

It was an old-fashioned garden of an old-fashioned inn. The blossoms of the spring azalea were resplendent in their beauty, yet they lacked the gorgeous coloring of the mountain blooms. Delicacy of tint was theirs, pure white and dim magenta or the even softer glow of a half-faded claret.

They flooded through the garden, did these blossoms of the Month of May, seeming like a spider web of gleaming silver gossamer in their moon-kissed whiteness or like glittering dewdrops touched into opalescence by the Queen of Night.

Gray lanterns of lichen and moss covered stone were half-revealed and half-concealed by this tangle of sweet blossoms. Lights from the other tearooms glittered through the flower-laden branches. Glimpses of the moon-loving lake that lay so close at hand yet seemed so distant wavered through them as the breeze that darkness brings in springtime swayed them gently into life.

The twanging of a samisen and voices raised in

laughing song floated through the opened shoji and out across the garden, sweeping into the dim-lit room, half out of doors and half within the house, where sat the listeners.

It was an old-fashioned inn with an old-fashioned garden, proud of its long history, living in the Past yet of the Present.

A thousand years and more ago this spot had been frequented by the children of the Isles of Sunrise. The temple to the Buddhist God of Fire that lies before us is an old, old temple, older by a century or more than the nearby capital of Dai Nippon. This was but a wilderness when Jikaku Daishi came from the lands of culture that are protected by Hiei-zan. Jikaku Daishi carved a spot of holiness from out the hillside and set up a fane of worship to the Buddha. Eastern Japan was still the haunt of barbarians in those ancient days. Slowly, resisting but powerless against their nemesis, the Ainu tribes were being driven northward. Strong and stronger from the south and west came the conquering pressure of the arms of Japan.

With sword and spear, with bow and arrow Yamato drove its course to north and east. In their wake, treading on the very heels of warriors, came the Buddhist priests. Altars to the God of India whom India has forgot were set up in this rude wilderness, grew and prospered.

With the coming of religion came the pilgrims. Where pilgrims gather anywhere, there do inn-keepers find revenue.

The God of Fire enshrined at this spot waxed famous, and the pilgrims grew in numbers. A day's, an easy day's—or quick night's—journey at that time from the site where Ota Dokan first constructed the moat-girdled stronghold that is now the Palace of the Emperor, Meguro was a village unto itself.

Other temples, other inns were built. Time passed, and with the passing years the primitive Kwanto was subdued, embraced, re-colored by the culture of Japan.

On through the centuries the pilgrims and the merrymakers trooped, threading the provinces, pausing for a night to pray before the great O Fudo Sama of this rustic Meguro and to riot in the inns and teahouses clustering about the temple's gate.

The Tokugawa came in all their power to make nearby Yedo the first city of the Empire. Poets and artists, interpreters of the posture-dancing of the No in peace and warriors of the plains and mountains when occasion called found homes and happiness and idle, pleasure moments in old Yedo. War drums were stilled, and in their place arose the tinkling samisen. Armor was doffed in favor of loose flowing garments. Art and the art of life flourished and bore dream-producing fruits. Once more was the Broad East subdued, embraced, re-colored.

While feudal lords whose forebears had borne sword and dagger stole out in secret to partake of the alluring pleasures of the capital, while merchants filled their coffers with the wealth that had been tribute once, and while all Japan save those in whom an ancient vengeance slumbered took its ease, this Place of Black Eyes, Meguro, still drew its pilgrims and its merry throngs.

Yet once again has the Kwanto been re-colored. Not from the Kwansai but from the truly Western World has come the influence that is now re-shaping an old Empire. Yedo is no more; Tokyo has been born. And Tokyo, ever changing, ever restless, has crept out and spread and grown until even once rustic Meguro has come within its embrace and though not as yet subdued will soon be so.

The pale moonlight sifted through the old-fashioned garden of the old-fashioned inn. From the temple of O Fudo Sama came the solemn, deep-reverberating tones of a bronze bell, struck by some acolyte or older priest. The blossoms of the white azalea trembled wistfully in response.

As the echoes of the bell sank into nothingness the petals of the more brilliant blossoms of the Month of May stirred into life, called into motion by the strains of samisen, by laughter and gay song that rang from out the tearoom across the tiny lake and garden.

> Yute shimao ka iwazu ni oko ka,
> Shian nakaba ni motsure gami?
>
> Should I speak it out or keep it unsaid?
> Tangled is my hair in the midst of indecision.

The dodoitsu that Yedo knew was being sung, and then a man's voice stilled the softer, sweeter notes, rising in strident tones of triumph first and then of entreaty. The rhythm of the dodoitsu that Yedo knew still broke upon the moon-enchanted garden, but the words that now rose and fell with its peculiar cadence told the tale of modern days, of the Kwanto that is the Kwanto of the Present, subdued, engulfed and conquered—first by the warrior, then by priest, once more by a refined aestheticism, and now by the West.

The pale moonlight sifted through the garden, gently caressing the azalea blossoms. The little lake was silvered into a dim glory by its beams. The Past joined hands with the Present in this old-fashioned garden of an old-fashioned inn.

Shinmiri

LAMB, in his "Dream Children," comes near to making understandable to the Westerner that most delicate, elusive and characteristic phase of Japanese emotional life which is termed shinmiri.

Yone Noguchi, in his rhapsody on the master-artist Hiroshige, exclaims as he drifts down blue waters under leafless branches of cherry blossoming trees at Mukojima: "I wonder if anywhere in the world but in Japan in spring one could have such a feeling as of drinking sadness from the cup of joy." Here is something of this element of shinmiri; here is much of it.

The pleasurable melancholy of slow rain dripping from warm eaves in a green garden may produce shinmiri. So may the cries of a cicada in the outer sunlight as one sits in the deeply shadowed recess of a temple grove of cryptomeria with the majestic trunks of stately trees rising straight and massive to support the lofty canopy of darkest green through which a ray or two of softened sunlight drops upon the wings of a brilliant, daring dragonfly.

Murmurs, shade and shadow, friendly leisure, a simplicity that brings content, that which sets the heart and soul instead of the brain a 'dreaming—these are needed.

Reverie is, perhaps, the nearest word we have in

English. Shinmiri is emotional; not primarily philosophical; it needs dignity yet it needs also homely friendliness. Action in tranquility, such action as the gently breathing, smooth, unbroken surface of the sea when winds are stilled, ripples through shinmiri. The thoughts drift slowly, "out of space, out of time." Their substance is the poignant substance of the mountain mists that enchant with their ethereal unreality yet stir to life the vagueness of half-understood longings which we do not seek to satisfy but rest content, enjoying pleasant discontent. Reverie, such reverie as Lamb's "Dream Children," is shinmiri.

To Japan shinmiri is a goal; with the West it is but incidental, unprovoked and seldom felt.

Japan's history is woven about her temples, tombs and shrines. The tiny garden of a Buddhist priest creates shinmiri. A fragile, black-winged butterfly with but a summertime for its whole life sips from the blossom of a thistle shaded by tall pines. The tiny, elf-like flights of song that are the poems of Japan spring from the pro-create shinmiri.

Shinmiri is the passive pleasure of the incomplete, of slight disorder in the midst of order, is the unsensed, unperceived factor in Japanese emotional aesthetics that enchants, yet baffles, us from out the West.

The Fragrance of Friendship

THE books of Old Japan are filled with romances where the long kimono sleeve of a maiden of gentle birth brushed that of a handsome youth in passing, and from this first slight contact which the myriad gods ordained sprang love and happiness, or love and tragedy.

We, the Westerners who choose to make our homes in the Empire of the Fartherest East, find many friendships with the Japanese if we but will. There are solid, comfortable friendships, based on the same grounds as are friendships in our homelands among our own people, friendships that are the bread and butter of life.

There are other friendships, friendships which endure in memory but which drift across experience for so brief a time that they have come and gone before we know it. Sometimes a moment or two suffices to reveal a truer glimpse of the heart of a man or a maid or of a race than would a lifetime of prosaic daily contact. As I have gone my way in Tokyo and in the green countryside of Japan there has drifted across my life, now and again, such a filament of gossamer, dewed with friendship and quickened into beauty by the sunbeams of the heart.

Chamé San

"CHAMÉ SAN," the waitresses at the little cafe called him, "Chamé San," which means Mister Mischievous Fellow.

He spoke slowly, lingeringly, as though enjoying every word and every word's effect. There was a glimmer in his eyes that was not quite the glimmer of mischief but perhaps we have no word in English that means just exactly Chamé San.

In his light summer kimono, open at the throat and dropping away from bared arms, he seemed the very embodiment of cool repose and ease those hot nights of July and August.

Everything about him, every action, every word or thought, was leisurely; and yet that is not quite the word. It was, rather, a timelessness and ignorance of haste, something of the reposeful dignity that is part of the concept of the aristocrat, for aristocrat he was throughout.

There was calm, measured dignity, yet genuine warmth of friendliness in the first few words exchanged. The chattering girl-waitresses were delighted. I, who dropped in occasionally at this secluded restaurant, was a high favorite with them merely because I was their only foreigner. And Chamé San had long since won their loyal friendship. How happy they were now that Chamé San and I were becoming friends.

Like brightly painted sparrows they fluttered about the table as we sipped our summer drinks.

Chamé San spoke English slowly, but no more slowly than his native tongue. He was a young interne at a nearby hospital. He had been graduated from one of Tokyo's many medical schools, from one of those which aid students to work their way and which, some times, when the necessity arises, find means to provide the sorely needed cost of education.

He was now an interne, an interne on a slender salary. His ambition was to go to America, to go to one of the great medical colleges of the United States. He could save a little money, but so very little, every month. And Chamé San sighed as his day-dreams drifted before his half-closed eyes.

I grew to know Chamé San better. We met now and then, sometimes at the restaurant, sometimes at other places. I took him once to the theatre, and there he met some three or four of my American friends. He won their hearts, as he won everyone's, with those reposeful, mischievous, dark eyes of his.

More of his tale unfolded as time went on. His home was in that bleak northern province that was known as Echigo in the days of samurai and battles. Thither had been banished all the most daring spirits of Old Japan. Any man so bold in Tokugawa times as to rear his head, to set his hopes too high, to be—in modern parlance—Liberal, was banished to its desolate shore.

The man of Echigo is different from the man of

the more protected provinces, and the difference is understandable.

His father, the descendant of that exile, was a merchant, for even exiled warriors had had to make a living somehow. He had an elder brother, and this brother liked the business, was content to settle down as tradesman, would carry on the family.

But Chamé San—he longed for nobler fields. The spirit of his banished samurai ancestors burned strong within him, as did their nobility of soul and charm of manners.

Chamé San came to my home for dinner one soft August night. For the first time I saw him clad in Western clothing. Trousers of white flannel and a darker coat, immaculate linen and the little touches of refinement all were his.

The dinner was American, for that was what I thought he would want. He ate his portion, and we moved back into the drawing room. His face was flushed, and I noticed a steadily growing anxiety of features, but never a betraying word. Finally he half-swooned, and I came to his aid. His belt was tight, so tight he could scarce breath. His collar choked him so that it was difficult to swallow.

And then, as he lay back on a chaise lounge and let the evening breeze revive him, the tale came out.

Never before had he donned foreign clothes, but tonight, he was going to the home of an American to eat American food, and his courtesy demanded that he meet the situation. From his slender savings destined in time to bring true that dream of an American university, had he taken enough to be properly clothed for his American host.

These things are done in Japan, in Japan where education means so much. It is not charity, but service to the State and to society. Slowly, as slowly as he talked himself, I persuaded him that I, too, knew the spirit of Japan, and that there was no thought of charity. Finally he capitulated, took me at my word.
Fifty sen for fifty sen, each yen for every yen that he deposited in the bank would be duplicated by me that he might the sooner go to school in the United States. It was to be a special fund, an account that could not be drawn on save for this one purpose.
"And how can I repay your kindness?" he asked.
Slowly, a dreaming smile spread over his face. "I shall give you," he said, "I shall give you one of the family swords."

I have never seen my laughing-serious Chamé San since that summer evening.
The account was opened, and was added to.
More than a month went by without our chance encounters, and then I sought him out.
"Oh, did not the Danna San know? Chamé San had returned to his native home."
Another week, and then the mails from Echigo brought me his letter. His elder brother, he who had been content to carry on the family and the business, had fallen ill. Chamé San had been summoned home, and his samurai soul did not question. The brother lingered on for a few weeks, suffered and perished.

Chamé San did not query fate. His duty was clear. Without a rebellious breath, but perhaps, with some dimming of those laughing eyes, he laid quietly to one side his dreams and his ambitions. The family, even the distasteful business, must be carried on, and he was now the eldest son. And so he wrote his Sayonara letter to his friend from out the West.

That was several years ago. In a bank of Tokyo, untouched and accumulating its small yearly interest, lies that beginning of a fund which was to have taken the smiling boy of Echigo to his land of dreams. It is his for the asking; but he has never asked.

Does he hope, perhaps, still to achieve his goal? Is it his samurai code of honor that forbids even the slightest perversion of a word once spoken?

Chamé San, even if he come to Tokyo on a fleeting visit will not call on me. His dignity would not permit it.

And I, bound to my round of toil that is usually a joyful service, can not go to distant Echigo. But if I could I would not. Unless the Wheel of Fate reverse somehow, Chamé San and I must remain forever for each other a vivid memory.

Gift of Poems

HE came wandering along the green lane to my home on the hill through the dusk of the summer evening, searching me out among the winding pathways of the great, rambling city of Tokyo. An eager smile spread over his young face as I stepped to the door, for he had found friend and sanctuary at last.

It was the hour of the evening meal, and I was to be with another friend that night.

With a happy sigh as though all problems were gone, he stooped to remove his shoes before entering the clean-matted house of Japan in which I dwell. There was no questioning in his mind of his welcome. Was I not his friend? Was he not in need of a friend? And now he had found me, everything was right once more.

It had been in that breathless space of time when the cherry blossom of Japan make of this world a heaven of sheer beauty that we had met. In the ancient capital of Kyoto, we had met beneath the blossoms of a temple garden misty in the moon-light and the clouds of falling cherry petals. We had strolled through the garden and had talked in our broken way, he using his few words of my language and I the few I knew of his.

The months had rolled by, to bring with them the

full tide of summer and with it his liberation from the classrooms of the university where he was a student.

He journeyed up to Tokyo. All through the heat of that July day he had wandered about the streets of the sprawling city, searching fruitlessly for a cousin. That cousin would take him in and give him food and shelter while he performed his pilgrimages among the sights of the capital. But the cousin was nowhere to be found. He had vanished completely, and the boy from distant Kyoto had no place to go, no spot in which to rest his tired body.

And then he remembered his friend from over the seas, and he sought me out in the cool dusk of the summer evening, sought me out in my home and my garden on the little hill that is like a secluded village of the countryside and seems far, far away from the dust and noise of the great city in which it nestles, half-hidden.

He was welcome, as welcome as he believed himself to be in his own simple, trusting faith. What heart would not have been touched by the repose of such confidence? And he entered the house with a happy smile. But I had to go then, and so he stayed behind to await my return.

A few hours later I pushed the gate with its bamboo clappers gently back in its grooves and entered the house. The lights were off, and my Kyoto comrade was sitting on the edge of the narrow little verandah, gazing into the moonlight-flooded garden and singing happily in contentment and rest.

He had prepared a gift for me.

In Japan all kindness is repaid with kindness. It

was not much he told me, for he had few possessions, but it was such a gift as is seldom accorded us of the busy, prosaic, Western World. As he had sat there under the light of the full moon of midsummer, at peace and protected after his day's wandering, his Japanese sense of the beauty of friendship had welled up and overflowed in poetry to me, his friend from a distant land:

>Dear friend,
>Far in an alien land,
>Who talked to me so lonesomely,
>I, too, share your feelings for home,
>And, gazing at the moon,
>I wish you "Bon Voyage!"

And then there had come back to him the remembrance of that flower-misted evening in the old garden of mountain-girdled Kyoto, where we first had met, and he wrote for me:

>'Twas an evening
>When the cherry blossoms on Ei-zan
>Had begun to fall
>As we roamed, talking,
>To the Chion-in,
>My alien friend and I
>Unexpectedly known to each other.

>The solitary moon
>Behind the pine branch
>Shed a hazy light.

>We were both away from home
>And instinctively heard each other
>Murmuring to the moon
>To comfort ourselves.

Non-Completeness

IT has been recognized, perhaps not generally but certainly among the more discriminating critics everywhere, that suggestiveness in literature is greater than is completeness.

As in literature, so in pictorial art. A painting, complete in itself, can not stir the imagination, the aesthetic sensibilities, as can one which completes itself in the mind and emotion of the beholder.

The Japanese long ago accepted this as a cardinal principle.

The picture always extends beyond its physical borders.

It is a partial glimpse; as is life.

The Western painting is nearly always complete within its own physical confines and then, as if to cap this completeness and drive it home relentlessly, it is framed in a broad, imagination-curbing frame.

The Japanese refuse to do this.

It is but one of the basic principles of their aestheticism, with its realistic symbolism, which, not being understood by an ututored Western World, is called elusive, mystic, even sometimes inscrutable.

The Earthquake-Dead

THE tinkling handbells of many pilgrims join this morning with the song of the uguisu and the fluttering petals of the blossoms of the plum in the chorus that welcomes the coming of the springtide that will triumph over snows on this day that marks the passing to the Other Shore of those who have gone on.

As the earth renews its beauty in response to the northward journey of the sun, the heart of Buddhist Japan inclines in reverent worship to the spirits of the dead. From the snow-clad Hokkaido to the flower-wreathed Okinawa the tinkling bells, the wooden drum or clappers and a thousand, thousand murmured prayers are heard before the Buddhist altar in the home and in the courtyards of the temples consecrated to that Faith.

Of all the temples of all Japan none touches the heart so deeply on this day of Higan as does that at Hifukusho-ato in Tokyo, where repose in peace and quietness the ashes of a near hundred thousand of the earthquake-dead.

Until the living honored these dead with a new and fitting temple, there was nothing heroic, nothing tragic, nothing even that was dramatic in the bare appearance to the eyes of Hifukusho; it was only in the heart. The drab sordidness and the dusty, uninspiring congestion that first followed the earthquake yielded to a pleasant cleanliness, and the decision was made to convert these seven acres of commonplace, temple-shack covered barrenness in the factory-tenement district of Tokyo east of the Sumida River into a green park and to rear there a shrine dedicated to All Religions.

There should be much about Hifukusho, other than mere thoughts, to impress the pilgrim and the visitor, for it is one of the most visited spots in all the world. The fire of incense lighted on the altar of the temporary temple there before the flames of earthquake-stricken Tokyo had flickered into ashes has never yet died out. Thousands of worshippers still throng there daily, each adding a bit of incense to feed the glowing embers. Its tragedy is enshrined in the hearts of hundreds of thousands, of millions. It is one of the most dramatic plots of ground in either hemisphere. But, until the new temple had been built, there was nothing dramatic in its physical appearance save the scarred trunk of a lone tree that endured through the scourge of life-taking fire.

On that hot September day when all Tokyo flamed with the fires of death, thousand upon thousand of the dwellers in Tokyo's overcrowded slum district fought their way through narrow streets piled high with household goods to the imagined safety of the open spaces of Hifukusho-ato, of the Military Clothing Depot that consisted of low rows of buildings edging a great common. Thirty-three thousand or more there were who crammed into this square, there to seek security.

There flames were not to be cheated. The typhoon

that swirled through the stricken city carried the fire across the broad stretches of the Sumida-gawa until its hungry tongues licked the little frame buildings and caught at the household treasures that had been carried to Hifukusho. An hour, two hours, three hours passed. Of what had been thirty-three thousand living persons, some scant twenty crawled from beneath the charred bodies of their comrades or out of the tiny lake in an adjoining garden—the only survivors.

Four days later, before the ashes of the capital had cooled, priests of the Nichiren sect of Buddhism raised an altar to the dead at Hifukusho and began the building of a crude wooden temple. A Shinto shrine followed, and a tent for Christian services, and temples of all the other sects of Buddhism. A wooden image of the Kwannon, the Buddhist Goddess of Mercy who looketh down upon the sound of prayer, one that was dedicated to All Religion, was placed in the temple. For a hundred days and a hundred nights masses for the dead were chanted without interruption.

Stalls for the selling of incense and picture postcards and flowers sprang up along both sides of the avenue leading to the temples that were but makeshift structures. The shuffling feet of thousands beat the ground into a fine dust that the wind picked up and scattered over all. The crowds were illy dressed and there were many odours, for of those who perished at this spot, most were of the poorer classes.

As a year, two years passed there came a change. The shacks that cluttered up the grounds were removed and a more dignified but still commonplace and temporary temple replaced the multitude of halls of worship. The ground was strewn with clean gravel, and a dark fence of palings shut off the central plot on which there was to be reared in future a temple-hall more fitted to the souls of those whom it sought to honor.

Commonplace though Hifukusho might be to the eyes, it could not be so to the heart. The thoughts that flood in as one stands on these seven acres where thousands met death in so brief a space of time can not be commonplace.

If one were courteous to the priest, the purple curtain that half-veiled the entrance to that temporary temple was lifted and the holy place itself entered. Before a simple altar of weathered-seasoned pine that bore its dedication to the dead were the offerings of cakes and flowers, and behind a second curtain lay the ashes of a hundred thousand, brought to this spot from wherever the earthquake and its attendant fires took toll of life. They were in neat boxes of clean metal, but when Japan greeted the first Higan after the great tragedy and the souls of these dead crossed to the Other Shore, a single room was filled with row on row of earthenware crocks and wooden boxes. Each was marked with the name of some district of the Kwanto and each contained clean gray ashes and tiny bits of charred bones.

There was nothing repulsive, nothing disgusting, in those clean gray ashes that had been human beings once. Here at last was the serenity and calm resignation of the Faith of Ancient India, of the Faith of Living Japan. From all over the great sprawling city and its environs, wherever man had met death that fateful first day of September, were these ashes brought. Some were taken to Koya-san, the sacred mountain where the saint and priest, Kobo Daishi, had founded his monastery more than a thousand years before, but most were left at Hifukusho.

It is right that these seven acres which have seen death piled on death so thickly now have been made into a park of green grass and tall, stately trees. Soaring from the center, rising from the spot where the charred trunk of that sole tree once stood, rises a shrine and mausoleum built by the contributions of the living. Its ground plan is that of a Christian cross, and it is crowned by the pagoda of Buddhism, and its simplicity is that of Shintoism, for this shrine transcends creed and dogma and is for the aching heart of all humanity.

A hospital for the relief of suffering, built by the free-will gift of Americans to a stricken people, stands behind the temple-shrine, and nearby is a great neighborhood hall for the use of the tenement dwellers of Tokyo, and adjoining that are the lovely gardens in which once stood the home of a millionaire but which he has now given to his fellow-men, the living and the living-dead.

Within this temple-shrine are kept the ashes of those dead, the clean gray ashes of those whose spirits will also hover near, as every Japanese knows. It is so much more fitting that they should be housed thus, rather than in the drab tonelessness and dreary mediocrity of those first temple-shacks they knew, a milieu that they would, in all probability, have known in the years to come as they moved about the tenements and factories of Northern Tokyo had death not levied so great a toll that hot afternoon and night of September.

True Tribute

TRIBUTE of a daimyo too poor in rice and lands to give aught else, the giant cryptomeria that stretch for miles on each side of the road leading to the Tokugawa temples at Nikko are the most lovely of all the many gifts of beauty offered by that gorgeous mountain shrine. Their great trunks stretch like pillars of some ancient colonnade from grassy banks that shut in the narrow, graveled roadway. Sunlight sifts through the dark green of their foliage to trace a delicate pattern of light and shadow in the dust.

They form an avenue, majestic, sombre, beautiful, that leads for many miles through the mountain country to the brilliant bridge of crimson lacquer arching over a tempestuous mountain stream, a bridge that only the Emperor or his messenger may cross. Beyond the bridge, under the dark shade of other cryptomeria, glitter the vermillion, gold and white of the overdecorated buildings erected to honor the first of the Tokugawa Shoguns. Their foil of green and black, with the dark gray of ancient stones, alone redeems the gorgeous coloring of man with the more lovely tones of Nature.

But the avenue of cryptomeria leads also into the heart of every Japanese. The memory of the daimyo who could not aid with gold the building of the mausolea and so set out these trees instead is a hallowed memory. The tribute that he rendered has become a treasure.

Asakusa Park

THE sweeping roof of the great temple to Kwannon blends into a double line of toy shops, topped by high tea houses that stretch out to the entrance of Asakusa Park. On the stone pavement of the narrow channel between the buildings flows and eddies a tide of kimono-clad humanity, now gathered about a tourist with opened camera, again surging about a brilliant display of dolls.

The clacking wooden sandals on flat stones form an undertone for the cries of the toy merchant, of the sidewalk silk seller and dealer in sweetmeats or hardboiled eggs. The steady murmuring of soft Japanese vowels and an occasional happy laugh merge into the sunshine that is a part of Japan.

Dolls—the samurai, the Court lady and now the Kewpie of the West —; drums and horns and samisen and mouth harps; tiny bits of ivory exquisitely carved and little miniature reproductions of all that man uses, so very, very small that they can be held on one finger; the bright silks and the brilliant, sparkling hair ornaments of geisha; roasted beans and peanuts, eggs heaped high with salt, pink colored ice and even ice cream, the gay and happy things of life make of this Street of Toys a joy and wonder.

The massive old red gate of the temple stretches

across the path, its giant paper lanterns hanging low. Through the gate pour pilgrim merry-makers for the Japanese is never too hurried to pause a moment before the Buddha, clap the hands, breathe a soft prayer and toss a coin into the coffers. Doves and pigeons, even chickens, flutter to a perch on the great lanterns of stone or come near the hand that is giving them grain. To the right is a Chinese pagoda; to the left across the trees lies the Street of Theaters.

Between this street and the temple, under bowers of wistaria and by the side of a little lake, the shops grow fewer and theaters and amusement halls more frequent, until, when the corner of the lake is rounded, there stretches out one long row of nothing else. As the lake is left the street again narrows and both sides are lined with theaters, their long, gay perpendicular banners nearly meeting overhead, their reds and blues and greens bearing curious Chinese ideographs, making a long vista down the aisle that seems to lead into the heart of Japan at play.

Sunset and Moonrise

THE great round disc of molten red and gold and purple was cut by the jagged mountain ridge that loomed through the mists of eventide across Lake Biwa. Rapidly at first and then more slowly the mountain with its uneven crest ate into the setting sun.

The train which bore us westward was merciful, for with its speed we were carried to a point that kept the sun the longer with us. But its descent was not to be stopped. Bit by bit the disc became a half-circle; then still less. Then thin branches of a single pine on the high skyline of the hungry mountain were silhouetted sheer against the sun itself. And then it dropped from sight.

At once the sky began to flame with a fiercer light. Purple and rose and gold, the splendor of the richest colors made still richer by their mistiness, covered the sky as if to compensate the loss of their lord, the sun. The bank-full rice paddies close by joined in the great chorus of worshipful praise, and ugly muck was turned to beauty by the glory of the heavens which they gave back from their still waters.

Across the valley near at hand the mists and vapors of the night began to rise. The panorama of the mountain range that rose peak on peak, long undulating ridge and sharper point, began to melt into the dusk. A fresh breeze stirred and paler, duller, deeper toned and darker grew the sky above the mountains. The glory paean of the spectrum of the sun died slowly, lingeringly, like a deep chord that has been torn from the heart of an organ. The day was done. Its monarch rested. And the sickle moon rose in the east to reign serenely through the night, keeping watch over the world for the orb from whom she draws her silvered life.

The Outcast

A SUDDEN gust of wind from out the west brought with it a great curtain of the warm rain of June, sweeping through the streets and enfolding in its wetness the languid strollers on the Ginza, out for a breath of the evening's air. The wind caught at the gay wares of night shops spread on low tables or the sidewalk pavement along the crowded, brightly lighted promenade of Tokyo. Catching the skirts of their kimono in both hands, the strollers galvanized themselves into quick life, running on clumping geta from the storm, scurrying about like little ants disturbed by the rude, unconscious breath of an invading giant, darting into doorways and through the portals of shops and restaurants, seeking refuge how and where they might.

A doleful cry went up from the itinerant shopkeepers as they strove to save their stock from damage. This seller of gay, colored toys of paper and bamboo saw his whole display melt into a sticky mass of running color and mere worthless trash before he had time to realize what was taking place. The vendor of apples, oranges and other fruits, laughed at his friend's discomfiture, for he knew that water would but make his own goods more attractive to the buyer.

Within the space of a few minutes the street that had been so gay with life and light and laughter was deserted. From the doorways of closed buildings little huddled groups looked out into the driving rain that cut through the night air, dimming the glow of electric bulbs, striking the glistening black pavement and dancing up and down in little puddles. Now and again a 'rikisha coolie, bent to the force of the wind, trotted laboriously through the storm, his doll-like carriage closed tight with curtains that its lucky occupant might be shielded from the night's punishment. Tram cars, so loaded that it seemed they scarce could move, crept down the center of the thoroughfare, their bells clanging, though no one ventured from his temporary shelter to cross the path of steel rails.

The bay corner window of the Lion Cafe, one flight above the street, that looked in three directions was a perfect coign of vantage for the watchers who had fortunately been caught beneath a roof instead of on the open street when first rain and wind swept in. Descending to the lower floor, the cafe was crowded with the refugees from the rain. Every table was occupied and the waiting public stood three deep around the walls. The tin-piano led orchestra was blaring forth with noise what was intended for the strains of "Rigoletto." The crowd, safe from an unwanted ducking, was in good humor, and the little waitresses were dodging in and out delivering tall glasses of amber beer crowned with collars of white foam.

"Rigoletto" crashed to a finish and another entertainer took the center of the floor. He, too, had sought the light and shelter of the restaurant when the storm had broken, but this gay room, gaudily decorated in red and green, with its crowd of respectable middle-class citizens and students, was not his element. He wore little more than a loin cloth, a torn dirty shirt clinging about his shoulders and falling below his waist, his legs and feet bare. But he was happy.

He was exhilarated, perhaps by the atmosphere but more so by the sake he had drunk. He wavered about among the tables, shouting greetings and laughing as the crowd good-naturedly laughed back at his queer antics.

It was to be expected that the two lone foreigners would catch his eye, and he came stumbling across the floor, bowing and nodding and calling honorable greetings to the strangers from a strange land.

He held out his hand, but as one foreigner, laughing himself in turn, grasped it, the derelict bowed deeply, placed the stranger's hand in both his own, and carried it humbly and respectfully to his forhead, murmuring in a few words of broken English: "You are very kind to me. I am an outcast, a Suiheisha, an —" he paused a moment and then spat out the hated word — "Eta!"

The crowd drew back and muttered something. The man turned, took the extended hand of the other foreigner and, again bowing deeply, carried it to his forehead, then straightened up and stood erect, proudly erect now and without a trace of drink, flung open the swinging doors and strode out into the storm.

Happiness in the Hakone

THERE is happiness in the Hakone again. For the first time in more than a year the smile on the face of khaki-clad chauffeur and the blue-coated peasant is not that of courage or of automatic courtesy but rather of sheer happiness and anticipation of the future. The sun is breaking through the thick clouds of hard times that since the Great Earthquake have hung over the Hakone, that region of mountains and valleys, of seashore, hot springs and the beauty of a beautiful land that is the playground for the dwellers in Eastern Japan and for many who come from far away to visit the Eight Great Islands.

Prosperity is to come with the dawning of the New Year, and for the first time since the tragedy of that tragic September the Hakone is to welcome back the hordes of city-weary denizens seeking open air and the freedom of the mountains, streams and lakes it holds out to them. With the thousands who will flock back to the Hakone for the five-day holiday by which the year is ushered in will go the gold and silver of the cities, gold and silver that are to remain in the mountains to pay for the new thatch on rebuilt cottage, the rice dumplings of the season, the deficit of many months' lean living.

There is a changed atmosphere like a freshening

breeze as soon as the train is left at Odawara. The hotel porter's smile is one that bubbles over; the chauffeur's greeting is the same. How different from only a month or two back before the Hakone knew when the tide would turn!

Through the narrow street of the town, swarming with children already at play with their New Year's kites and battledores and shuttlecocks, there is this spirit of optimism. Odawara suffered in the earthquake and the fires that followed, suffered in proportion more greatly than did Tokyo. Like the capital, the town has been rebuilt. New homes and shops have been erected, but scant trade has come to them. The whole district is like one family, its interests interwoven and depending for their sustenance upon the money brought in by visitors. And there have been no visitors, only the few who have defied the broken roads and marched afoot over mountain trails to their destination. But now the stream of guests, Japanese and foreign, is to set in once more, and Odawara is singing gaily these bright December mornings.

Twelve months ago the Hakone was a folorn and desolate place. For the last four miles that lie below Miyanoshita it was necessary to walk up a narrow path, all that was left of the old motor road, while the hills crumbled above and below as the thaw followed the freeze. The Hakone had not then settled down. Earth tremors came each day, and with each major shock a bit more of the mountainsides went tumbling toward the sea.

The new motor road now stretches from the level coast at Odawara up through the twisting gorge to the crest of the Hakone Mountain range where it passes through a tunnel to emerge with the full grandeur of Fujiyama rising dead ahead, or, if the other branch be taken, swings around a corner into space with the amethystine jewel of the Lake of Reeds gleaming in its setting of green hills below. The new road is better than the old, is broad, well built, well surfaced and enduring. Already the creeping electric line that tunnels through the cliffs is once more in operation.

On that trip a few years ago the Fujiya was not open, but its host took in his weary guests and made them warm and comfortable, fed and cared for them as best he could. The shops that deal in curios and in the porcelains and silks of Japan were but half-repaired. Their owners were a disconsolate lot. They had lost heavily in the earthquake; what was more appalling, they had lost their trade. For many months less than a dozen customers had visited them.

Today as one winds upward through the groves of bamboo and of pine, past waterfalls that break in spray, gazing down on the mountain torrent in the gorge below or upward to the heights, across great stretches of bleak, barren soil where the earth broke loose, sunshine and gaiety are all around. It is the old Hakone, the Hakone of the happy pre-eathquake period, changed somewhat in physical appearance by Nature but unchanged in the nature of its smiling courtesy.

The peasants on the road step to one side to let the car slide past, calling a simple greeting of good will. The workmen from Korea rebuilding the electric line gaze at the motor with a grin. A carter thanks the chauffeur for his consideration in giving the slower horse-drawn vehicle the inner side of the road.

At the Fujiya, now a blaze of fresh paint and cleanliness, the explanation comes. Already, weeks in advance, every room in the vast, rambling structure with its many gardens, waterfalls and beauty spots has been booked for the New Year season. The Fujiya epitomizes the Hakone, is the "head of the family." As with it, so with the many Japanese inns that dot the mountains. With a full hotel and inns, the dealers in curios know that their empty coffers will tinkle again to the sound of coins. With many visitors, the chauffeurs know the company, their company, will pay the New Year's bonus. With guests from other cities once more in the district, the fishermen, the orange growers and the farmers know the market for their produce will return once more. There is happiness in the Hakone again. Even through the dreary work of waiting and rebuilding there have been smiles, smiles of courage, but the smiles today are those of happiness.

There is no other district like unto the Hakone, where each man works to help the other, where all are members of one family. The Fujiya is the head; the Japanese inns the elders; the people are the children. The owners of the inns hold stock in the Fujiya; the owner of the Fujiya stock in the inns. The motor car company operates throughout the district, and each chauffeur owns an interest in it. He is working for himself, and his brother chauffeur is working for himself, too, and each is working for the other, and all are working for the hotel and the Japanese inns of the mountains and valleys, and the hotel and inns are working for the motor company in which they share and working to help each other's business which is also, in some measure, their own, and even the dealers in curios and the farmers are in this league whose object is to give such willing, pleasant service to the visitors.

The chauffeurs are sons of the Hakone by birth. The child playing in the road as the great car sweeps by may be the chauffer's son or nephew. The carter who draws to one side of the road to let the powerful motor rush past may be but giving the open way to his brother's or his cousin's or at least his neighbor's son at the wheel. The farmer laboring in the rice paddy raises his eyes to see some friend or relative employed at this or that inn acting as guide to the inn's guests. Everywhere, throughout the length and breadth of the Hakone, one is in the bosom of a family and of a most happy family once more.

When It Is Cold

As dusk falls over the sprawling city of Tokyo these cold winter evenings the jingling of little bells and the cry of "Rokkon Shojo" may be heard rising on the frosty air. Japanese youths, clad only in a single short garment of thin white cloth belted at the waist, run hurriedly through the streets of the capital, converging on one of several popular temples dedicated to O Fudo Sama, the Buddhist God of Fire.

Arrived at the temple, they remove even their scanty garments and stand in the freezing cold, pouring bucket after bucker of cold water over their heads and naked bodies. A short service in worship of the deity follows, and then they don their simple slips and once more set off on a run through the city to their homes, ringing their hand-bells, carrying lighted paper lanterns and uttering their religious implication.

They are the young men who are about to be apprenticed to one trade or another, and this ordeal is in preparation for their future success. The hardening of the body to cold weather and the moral courage needed to perform this feat are considered requisites of a good apprentice for the years to come.

Nor are the devotees confined to men. More than one girl born in an old-fashioned family practices the same austerities, although the temple baths are closed to them in the evening. Other young girls who desire to obtain the benefit of the rite but are unwilling to brave its unpleasantness merely visit the temple of O Fudo Sama and there pray for success.

It is only during the Sho-kan and the Dai-kan, the periods of Little Cold and Big Cold, that this ordeal is practiced.

The Snow Comes

THE sky—gray, murky and too close to earth—gave promise that mid-winter morning of the long-delayed snow so panted for by sickness-stricken Tokyo. The wind blew from the north, cold and fresh, the breath of the snow-covered lands over which it had rushed in its swift passage giving a tang and zest to life that belied the gloom of the gray skies.

The waters of the bay seethed sullenly in one great mass, unbroken by a foaming whitecap, untouched by the gold of even one stray sunbeam. Rifts of the thick fog of early morning lingered here and there, clinging with tenacious stickiness to low-lying spots and outlining the dirty meandering canals of the city burdened with humanity polling slow-moving barges deep in the water from their heavy loads. A tiny flame from charcoal glowed on each weather-beaten deck, for it was the hour of the morning meal. A slattern woman, slack breasts half-bared regardless of the cold, prepared the simple breakfast of Japan's lower classes.

One knew that Fujiyama, as shy of self-revelation as any beauty of the Court, lay to the southwest, one knew that the mountain's white perfection pierced the gray bank of clouds, but Fujiyama did not deign to show itself to its multitude of worshippers. The lower, nearer mountains stood out in black splotches against this all-pervading grayness.

Those who must toil and work scurried about the dank streets, their coats drawn close drawn against the chill cheerlessness. Bleak monotone was king.

Silently, giving no warning, from the dull sky there fluttered toward the thirsty ground the first few flakes of snow. Bared hands were stretched our eagerly to feel its chaste coldness, and eyes swang upward hopefully.

The flakes came faster, joined by comrades in adventure in increasing numbers. The ground began to whiten. At first it was like a thin frost, only the slightest of gauzes spreading over the earth. The soft storm grew rapidly. The snow displaced the fog and filled the air with a moving opaque, silent waterfall of frozen crystals; thick and more thickly fell the flakes; the whiteness of the snow was wedding earth and clouds into a oneness, tangible, unreal yet semi-solid.

On through the darkened daylight hours, darkened to the sun and yet taking from the falling shower of whiteness a strange eerie light that was macabre, beat the storm. Cased within walls in which a sickly electricity prevailed, the gaze turned ever through the window pane, toward the street and the dark waters of the moat beyond.

With slender body bent like an archer's bow, a maiden bowed to the power of winter as she pushed through the blinding, snow-filled air. Her umbrella of oiled crimson paper was but half unfurled. Holding it above her black lacquered locks as if it were both shield and spear she pushed onward. Her geta sank into the drifts in noiseless rhythm. Her sober outer skirts tucked high, a scarlet petticoat gleamed from beneath, revealing now and then a bared leg as the wind flicked back this slight protection.

His brown legs twinkling in a steady running stride, a 'rikisha man curved into the blast his mushroom-hatted head and upper body to draw his black-curtained carriage through the semi-twilight.

The day waned. The half-hearted bulb of man-made light gained strength as the world darkened out of doors.

Long before its due time black night enveloped all the world, black night through which the silent snow continued on its now invisible and always silent mission of blanketing with beauty the ugliness that sunshine pricks into sharp relief.

As the next day dawned, the golden sun rose from out the restless waves of a black ocean. Its beams struck through the opened shoji, claiming the attention of the sleeping dreamer. Their clear rays fell upon a world of beauteous glory that the storm had wrought.

At Matsushima

A NARROW strip of beach, carpeted with dank sea-weed when the tide is out, bordered and held in place by a low wall of wave-washed stones, forms the frontage for a long line of inns and shops that are the little town of Matsushima. Between the inns and the sea there stretches a wide grass-covered village green in fact, welcome relief in an overcrowded Empire where few bits of soil fitted to the nation's farming are let rest in peace and idleness.

The shops and inns are background, the quiet waters of the island-dotted bay the foreground, for the life of the villagers, the tourists and the pilgrims to this northern hamlet. Squeaky steamers dock at the miniature pier, side-wheelers that play to nearby islands and to Shiogama on the mainland. The junks of fishermen and motor boats of visitors are tied to iron rings or posts of stone set in the seawall. Stark naked children and their elder brothers with but little more apparel splash about in the waters, delighting in the rippling waves created by the passing boats. The sun beats down upon their sun-browned bodies as they shout and laugh in pleasure.

Standing out to sea, scattered among the pine-clad islands with their low sepia cliffs of soft sandstone, the square-cut sails of fishing boats drift lazily about at the dictation of the gentle breeze. To the right the slender curve of a red painted bridge arches from a promontory to the little island of Oshima with its burned temple, caves and time-worn carvings in the rock.

The isle of Oshima is one of many gems that are scattered loosely in the more prosaic setting of the village and its round of daily life. The Kanrantei, the "Seeing Waves House," is another. It, too, is old, as age is reckoned in the West. More that three centuries ago the simple house was built upon its little cliff that looks across the waves, and a great artist painted in gold and green and other colors the screens that make the walls of a room prepared for the visit of the Taiko, of the warrior whose sword carved out, ironically, the basis for the rearing of the Tokugawa's power and the armed peace that held the feudal lords of Old Japan in unity. Meiji Tenno, too, the Emperor of Great Enlightenment who had but ascended the Throne when Perry came, has slept in the Kanrantei. His son and his son's son, the present Emperor, have been here.

Three bridges lead to the Hall where Five Deities are enshrined, to the Godaido, which looks out across the waters and the islands to the south. Zuigan-ji, a temple of the Buddhist Faith where the Date clan are reverenced, set in a grove of cryptomeria with a lake of blossoming lotus nearby, is another of these loose-flung jewels of Matsushima.

More lovely than the work of man, unspoiled except in part by human hands, is the bas-relief of land and water made by Nature. Low hills garbed in pine and bamboo rise near the shore. The jagged coast line has been carved and cut, indented, broken off in bits by wind and wave. Barred from the blue ocean by its protecting chain of islands, the blue bay ripples peacefully, embosoming other islets with their crowns of pine trees that make the name of Matsushima—Pine-clad Islands.

All this for background-foreground. But no artist of Japan will paint a picture, carve a woodblock print, that lacks a human figure or at least the signs of man's habitation.

Coast resorts are of a pattern everywhere. Their details differ; that is all. Japan differs from the West in some respects; each spot within Japan is slightly different from its fellows. And yet, the stage carpenter, the stage painter, whose work it is to reproduce with board and canvas Matsushima or some similar spot needs rare genius to introduce the touch of individual distinctiveness.

The long line of glass-walled, weather-darkened buildings that fronts on the village green might well be the back-drop at the Kabuki-za. Their lower floors are shops; their upper storeys are all inns for those who seek the coolness of the coast in summertime. Girls in blue kimono with their skirts tucked high and showing scarlet under-robes beneath stand at the open shop-fronts calling forth their wares, entreating every passerby with Irasshai, to Enter Here. Towels, stamped with pines in deep blue ink, shells and fantastic ornaments of shell, wind-bells of metal tinkling merrily in the breeze, bamboo canes and bamboo seals, conches and carved wooden trays and picture postals, even cases made of whale skin in this northern land are all on sale. Few tempt the Westerner.

In the restaurants of this modern day gaudy posters flaunt the virtues of some brand of beer, and the young waitress chaffs with her young patron at the table. A stream of white-clad pilgrims with wide sun-hats of straw troops by, for in Matsushima the pilgrim garb of other days is still predominant and has not yielded precedence to Boy Scout uniforms as at Nara and on Hiei-zan.

As night falls the softest of pink glows is caught and mirrored in the east, while the quiet bay in turn reflects the light and color that the hills upon the west have sought to hide. Lights gleam along the shore. In the fading twilight three men pose upon the beach before a camera. Incongruous, grotesque almost, they stand self-conscious in stiff attitudes and stiffer smiles. One wears coat and shabby trousers, a straw hat; another is more dignified in the tight-buttoned uniform of his business firm; the third has already shed his daily clothes and wears only the broad-striped kimono furnished by the native inn for sleeping garment, which bulges at the waist where he has stored tobacco pouch, his purse and what not else. The picture will be prized—by them; and by their families.

As if but waiting for the eventide the inns and restaurants pour forth their troops of men and women. Arm in arm, two students stroll along the beach. Laughing and chatting gaily, a little waitress and her servant-lover pass. The children shout at play, rollicking about the open space or dipping strong, bare toes into the waves. All eyes turn to watch the progress of a geisha from the capital in silken garments and with perfumed coiffure. A long boat propelled by a single sweep at the stern is ready to set out. Red lanterns bob at each end as its merry-making occupants clamber in and push off to join other parties on the water and to weave in and out among the lanterns of the fishermen whose work is not completed.

The bay is dotted with these fairy points of light, while now and then a flare against the sky that makes one think of kitsune-bi, or ghostly fox fire, shows above some island. "Yoi, yoi, yoi," comes the chorus from a boat, followed by clapping hands. "Yoi, yoi, yoi"— it is echoed back from the land, echoed by the villagers and visitors who have deserted their village for the public park in which stands the foreign hotel. Singly, in pairs, in groups they stroll about the park, now pausing for a moment on some bench or resting on the grass. On into the soft August night they talk and laugh and sing. What need of care? of worry? To-morrow, perhaps; this is tonight, is tonight upon the Bay of Matsushima lit by the stars, cooled by the evening breeze, sung to by low-lapping waves.

The Ginza

"GINBURA" is the term in Japanese especially coined for a stroll along Tokyo's principal street—the Ginza. To take the evening breeze in the summer is rated as one of the pleasures of life by the people of this Empire, and of all the places to take it none is considered superior in Tokyo to the Ginza. In the ancient capital of Kyoto, where life is more tranquil and is more beautifully lived, a warm summer night finds the bridges and banks of the Kamogawa, the clean river that cuts through the heart of that city, lined with hundreds and hundreds of strollers or of people sitting and laughing in the half-boat, half-pavillion cafes wide open to the air erected there for the summer season. In Tokyo, they go to the Ginza.

Always, each night, throughout the year, the Ginza is thronged.

And so, one mid-July, when the white stone Shimbashi, the New Bridge, was dedicated, it was almost impossible to thread one's way through the slow moving masses of humanity. The Shimbashi stands at the western end of the Ginza, the new "New Bridge" replacing the old which was so badly damaged by earthquake. For many months traffic was detoured to other streets while stone masons and other workmen labored on the bridge that spans the dirty canal which once formed the outermost moat of the Shogun's castle-home. It was cause indeed for celebration when the bridge was completed, and the true Yedokko, the children of Tokyo, the children's children of pre-Tokyo, seldom overlook a chance to make merry.

Arches gaily painted and decorated were erected at the approaches to the bridge, and the whole of the neighborhood was dressed for the holiday in brilliant bunting and paper lanterns of the land. Flimsy platforms were erected for the use of vagrant street actors and for dances by the geisha of the Shimbashi district, among the most famous geisha of the capital. Great bales of rice and kegs of sake were heaped higher than the heads of passers-by, and firemen, the traditional guardians of the Yedo Spirit, were moving about garbed in the picturesque clothes of other days and carrying iron rods crowned with jangling rings of metal with which they vainly sought to guide the traffic.

Tokyo, a city of many millions, is in truth but a vast group of villages that have grown together with the passing years, and each little district that was once an independent village still retains its local pride. In no other place is this more true than in the Shimbashi, which, despite the fact that it is part of the modern business district now, seems to preserve its links with the past in unusual degree. It was almost like stepping back into pre-Meiji days to mingle with the crowds celebrating the dedication of the Shimbashi.

Almost, not quite. The kimono of the geisha, the masks of the street-actors, the firemen and the anachronistic decorations are the Japan of other days. But not the buildings like unto those of New York that rear close at hand and that tower in the distance.

Nor yet the throng of people crowding about for the celebration, some of whom wear kimono but more are clothed in coat and trousers.

The Ginza starts at the Shimbashi and runs northeastward a few blocks, paralleling the bay. The Ginza is, itself, but a few blocks long and gains its name from the fact that once a silver mint stood there, but the dwellers in Japan who have come out of the West insist on dubbing several miles of street by the name of the Ginza. No other spot in Tokyo has received as much attention from visiting writers, for whether it be summer or winter, whether daytime or at night, in rain or in sunshine or in moonlight, the Ginza always interests and frequently entrances. It has been said and most well said, that in the development of the Ginza is mirrored in miniature the growth and development of Modern Japan.

It was in the early days of the Meiji Era that Viscount Tsuyo Mishima granted permission to the petty merchants of rechristened Tokyo to hold fairs along the Ginza. In those days the street was no more than a dirty, deserted corner of a sleepy city, lined with low buildings of wood and tile. Acrobats, tiny theatres, men with performing monkeys, story tellers and other public entertainers flocked to the Ginza when the fairs were held. The merchants set up little booths along the roadway or spread their wares on the ground each night, the scene being lit by the glow of myriad paper lanterns. Cheap toys, old furniture, even an odd agricultural implement or two were to be found on sale, in addition to many, many trinkets and curios.

Prosperity came to the Ginza with its night shops

beneath its waving willow trees. New and better buildings were erected, buildings of red brick trimmed with white stone. Glaring electric lights replaced the dimmer lanterns of rice paper. A tram line was built down the center and the street was paved—but not without violent protest from the conservatives.

With surprising rapidity Japan continued to convert itself from a feudal, mediaeval nation into a modern Power, and the change was mirrored from year to year by the aspect of the Ginza.

Then came the earthquake and the fires of 1923. The Ginza was levelled from end to end, left a blackened waste. Only the steel and concrete skeletons of the larger buildings still stood erect, but they, too, had been gutted by the flames, Overnight, desolation replaced prosperity.

Almost overnight, also, did prosperity return. No spot in the devastated capital was more quickly rebuilt than was the Ginza. The skeleton structures still left were reconditioned. Temporary shops of wood and corrugated iron, fantastically designed and many of them hideously ugly, were run up with amazing speed. The Ginza came back into its own, and for the third time had changed its dress within the memory of living man.

Not only did the Ginza come back into its own, but it began to make great strides to further triumphs. Six and seven and eight storey buildings and department stores have been built. Retail firms located elsewhere are opening branches on the Ginza. Development is feverish. The Ginza Merchants Guild is considering great plans. A loan of many millions may be sought in America with which eight-storey buildings, each a block or half-block wide, will be built to replace existing less important structures. It was no idle remark made long ago that in the Ginza may be seen reflected the development of Modern Japan.

And in the life of the Ginza, in the crowds that throng its sidewalks and that shop in its stores or make merry in its cafes is present-day Japan to be found in its fullness. The night shops with their wares spread on the pavement still attract and interest, but not as does the stream of humanity that passes by.

The millionaire in his motor car rolls down the center of the street, pausing to look at this or that work of art. Workmen scantily clad in these days and nights of heat, wander about laughing and enjoying the rest that comes with the end of the day's labor. A little mother with her baby bound securely to her back trips along and gazes with admiration at the lovely kimono worn by a group of geisha who are out to take the evening air. Students, some with the square cap that denotes the universities and others with the round cap of the lower schools, strut or swagger or walk sedately, each to his own temperament. Haikara San, the Japanese youth who seeks to be as the youth of New York and who is dressed in the latest fashion of Broadway, is here in abundance, as are his still more modern cousins, the Mobo and the Moga, the Modern Boy and Modern Girl. It is, indeed, their happy hunting ground, for on the Ginza they can see and be seen, and why dress in style if not for the eyes of others?

From the cafes there come loud bursts of laughter and on this corner stands a street musician, twanging away at his whining instrument for the sake of stray coins that may fall in his outstretched cap.

To some who take the evening air the Ginza means hilarity and boisterousness; to others it is still the quietly subdued pleasure that was felt in days gone by, that is felt still in Kyoto but is more elusive in this modern capital of Tokyo with its strange incongruities of East and West in juxtaposition but so seldom in harmony. The development of Modern Japan is indeed mirrored in miniature by the Ginza.

From Peking to Tokyo

Peking to Mukden

DAWN crept over the plains to sketch in sharp detail the world of glistening white and barren brownness that is North China in the winter season, for a heavy hoar frost lay on every twig and branch and dried, dead blade of grass. The deep, thick carpet of dun-colored dust that swirls into the capital of Kublai Khan in driving yellow clouds in March and April was subdued by the cold moisture of the February morning.

The bleak stretches of the Metropolitan Province of old Chihli seemed to move in broken, silent waves until they reached the blue-gray of the horizon. Nearby the skeleton of a tree that would live again with the coming of spring rose above the monotony of visible space. Its intensely black trunk startled, for the pure whiteness of the frost that wrapped each tiny, delicate twig had made a fairy bower of all the branches, a robe of beauty for a tree that not even the pink cherry blossoms of Kyoto or the glowing scarlet maple leaves of Nikko can surpass. Perhaps a grove of trees formed one great fleecy Heaven beneath which lay the brown mud walls of huts that China's millions call their homes. Across the dusty stretches moved a blue-covered Peking cart or mule with jingling bells and warmly padded rider. The trees far off had taken wings, and the whiteness of their branches floated silently above the edge of earth like tiny clouds or wisps of smoke.

The clear sky and the brown vastness of the level lands of weariness that stretch from Yangtze Kiang to Amur were redeemed. The cruelly skillful hand of Northern Winter had produced a masterpiece.

Mukden to the Korean Border

Hills rose on every side. Not glorious mountains like the Matterhorn or Fujiyama, but bare hills, bleak with the northern winter of Manchuria, scarred with the traces of great storms, brown, earthy-dead and dull, the surface of an aged land that shows its age.

The line of steel that represents the progress and the penetration of Japan swept inland from the coast. The silent, barren hills looked on. In years long gone they gave the birth to Manchu sons and sent them forth to conquer China and the East. This modern squirming creature, made of metal, breathing steam and battling time, swung through their bowels and triumphed forth its victory. The hills looked on. They were unconquered. Their silence was the silence of all time and the sure knowledge of their own great past; their grandeur that of calm indifference. If come the Islander then come he must, but conquer never. His borings through the surface of the soil cut deep but do not kill. His torii and his Shinto shrine can not drive out the temple of Confucius. This land is Manchu, and the Manchus are the Lords of China.

Seoul to the Sea

The mists hung low. Across the gray expanse of

last year's terraced rice fields, silvered by the frost, rose mountain chains, their peaks so dimly seen they melted into soft gray clouds of Heaven.

A pile of brush, so large it blotted out the mud hut of its peasant owner, came slowly down the narrow, twisting road, and looking close, one saw an ox moved patiently beneath.

The door of the mud hut swung back. With all the dignity of all mankind there stepped from out this squalid home of dirt a farmer-nobleman. His head was high, his step had the calm majesty of Emperor, his pure white garments were unsoiled and tiny, light blue ribbons at his ankles fluttered in the wind. Silent he stood a moment, then again he moved with that same calm, majestic grace that is the birthright of the Sons of Morning Calm. He, too, was burdened with a load so great it blotted out his home—his country was not free. The tragic pathos of futility and simple pride were in his stately progress down the narrow road of earth.

Entering the Harbor of
  Shimonoseki at Dawn

On into the mists that shroud the Islands of Japan we crept. Two great black walls of rock reared high for us to pass between. The silver spray our bow cut from the water melted into darkness. A beacon light gleamed out. Another flashed from far beyond a mountain top, the outer gateway to the Inland Sea, where daimyo and old samurai had given battle to the Western World.

On, on we crept. The mists paled into gold, to ruby red, to crimson and to sunlight. Queer shapen junks in all the glory of the Fartherest East stood out. The high rock walls changed into pine tree laden mountains. An old, old Japanese and his bare, bronze-limbed son stood on the side of fishing smack and clapped their hands into the east, for the glory of the Great Sun Goddess shone once more on the fair Sun Rise Isles of Old Japan.

Through the Inland Sea

The amethystine girdle of Japan, jewelled with myriad emerald islands and encrusted with the gold of sunshine, lay on both sides. Orange grove and thicket of bamboo, the first year greenness of the untransplanted rice and tender mulberry or tree of tea half hid and half revealed the blue kimono and the broad straw hat of peasant girl at work.

Across life-giving fields of mingled soil and water rose the hills. The slope grew steep, then merged to terrace gray of lichened-covered stones on which there lived the wonder of a Buddhist temple or the slender, graceful arch of beauty-loving, sovereign-worshipping Japan.

Kobe-Kyoto to Tokyo

We sped along low-lying shore line, fringed with palm and pine, from which there led the rock-strewn, warrior beds of mountain streams across the flat rice paddies to the heights. Here under heavy thatch stood weather beaten boards or creamy plaster of a peasant home. Glimpses of mountain, plain and sea, and then we turn into the mountain range that men have christened the Hakone.

On up and up; the plain becomes a narrow valley

filled with pines and bamboo groves through which there races a clear, sparkling brook past orange groves and through mossed wooden water wheels. The valley narrows more; great clouds and mists roll back and far above there towers in the vast majesty of sacred awe the glory of Mount Fuji, The glistening snow-white purity is touched by sunlight, and men comprehend the wonder of sublime perfection.

Bearers of Wood

LIKE a procession of gnomes from out some weird tale of other days they came. Wending their way slowly upward, bent almost double by the great packs of faggots on their backs and with curiously crooked sticks on which they leaned, they toiled slowly up the twisting mountain road which was crumbling all about them. Snow lay on either side and weighted down the branches of the pine and cryptomeria, but the narrow road was muddy, muddy as only Japan can be muddy.

The little women, for they were women with the skirts of their drab kimono tucked high above their knees, passed silently and uncomplainingly in review. They were carriers of wood, and if discontent slumbered in their shrunken bosoms it showed not in their passive faces. If ambitions and dreams and aspirations lay stifled within them, there was no outward sign as they stolidly did their day's work, as stolidly as they had done it the day before and the day before that and as stolidly as they would do it tomorrow and through all the tomorrows to which they were bound by the Wheel of Life.

Far From Echigo

THE curious juxtaposition, so vastly different from a true mingling, of the East and West was in full evidence in this cafe of present-day Japan. It was a popular cafe in a popular district—the most popular cafe in the district most frequented and liked best by those seeking diversion in the most populous city of Japan. There were other, far more entrancing restaurants in this district, restaurants that were purely Japanese in every way, in the style of architecture, in the food they served, in the atmosphere sought and obtained in full adherence to the Japan that is vanishing. But this was the most popular cafe in a district that for centuries has been marked off, set apart, become and remained individualistic among a people in whom non-standardized standardization has been bred.

The floors of this cafe were concrete; the heating was by coal stoves with tin pipes scattered at too distant intervals; the decorations were the gorgeous maple leaves of autumn but the season had already passed the New Yeartide. In the more charming, lovelier restaurants of Old Japan this would have been blasphemy, but where the West is called in as the dominant motif who is there so bold as to uphold the aestheticism of the cha-no-yu, who so bold as to claim that the dictates of classical good taste should be observed?

There were students, a few workmen out of place and many, many clerks scattered about the cheap, overvarnished tables, seated in stiff, uncomfortable chairs. A few, perhaps a half a dozen, were clad in the kimono of Japan; the vast majority wore the garments of the West.

They wore them well.

A brief twelve years ago only the returned diplomat or the business man who had dwelt long in Western lands could wear a coat and trousers, vest, necktie and "high collar" from abroad and still look neat and trim. Then, there was a strong, a very popular song, which rang along the streets of Tokyo.

Iyada, iyada yo, Haikara San, iyada.
I hate, I hate, High Collar San, I hate you.

Haikara San is the Japanese youth dressed in the style of Broadway, Picadilly. Was it envy, malice, hatred, contempt, an unattainable longing, that provoked this song? One wondered.

Haikara San is no longer a lone, isolated figure, gazing into some shop window along the Ginza to catch his own reflection and then sally forth defiant, yet at heart so diffident, to face the taunts of fellow-countrymen. Haikara San now dominates the cities, and, even, has invaded the countryside, long sacrosanct to the conservatives, as the Japan of art, aestheticism, leisure flees before our eyes. He has even changed his nickname; he is now known as Mobo.

The strange juxtaposition, that is so different from a true mingling, was crystallized in this restaurant that drew the crowds away from quiet rooms covered with the clean rice-straw mats of Old Japan. The overvarnished tables and the faded maple leaves still blossoming in January, the sparsely scattered men in blue kimono and the overbearing presence of Haikara San, the flirting waitresses and the whole atmosphere were but contrast for that which was to come.

Stooping behind his bar where no customer could see, a homesick Boy San from the countryside drew forth his poor harmonica, treasured gift from parents when he had left his home. He touched it lovingly, caressingly, his fingers almost reverent and his eyes filled with the dreams that make this life worth living. Slowly, but not reluctantly, he raised the simple instrument to his half-parted lips.

And then, gently as the sunset's reflected afterglow fades from the eastern sky at evening, he breathed into this mouth harp that meant to him Japan because he had been born since that short time ago when it, too, was foreign.

The pulsating rhythm of the Lion Dance of Echigo came softly yet with all-pervading emphasis from the hidden player. It swelled and ebbed, became triumphant and then tremulous, until those few among the curious crowd who were attuned could see and feel the presence and could sympathize with that long-gone wanderer who first danced this Lion Dance on the lonely beach of Echigo along the bleak northern coast of the sea that sweeps between Japan and Russia, wringing from his heart the longing for his missing love.

Gone was the gaudy restaurant, gone was the

noisy, maudlin crowd, gone was all thought, of the present as the listener drifted with the lonesome player into the day, the years, the centuries that live now but in romance.

The spell was broken, broken rudely, suddenly and wantonly as New Japan is prone to do.

From the cheap piano on the other side of the concrete-floored restaurant blared forth in strident tones the notes of "Home Sweet Home."

In other places, touched by a master's hand, this melody will stir such memories and nostalgic longings as had been stirred to life by the breath of the hidden harpist. But not here, not when the keys are pounded by someone to whom it is no more than a tune from out the West, a goal toward which Young Japan is striving, an all too evident hallmark of what to these Haikara San, these Mobos spells civilization.

The soft notes of the hidden player wavered into an involuntary tremolo, broke, and died. Slowly and with a twisted smile of pathos he lowered his simple instrument of dreams. Lovingly, but with the touch of surrender, he wiped the mouth-piece wrapped it once more in its bit of silk, and thrust it deep into his bosom.

The piano grew more strident, swelled into a misplayed jangle that compelled attention from the boys and men seated at the overvarnished tables, and from the aproned waitresses. Hands beat in unison, and, as the pianist flourished to the end, there rose a heavy round of undeserved applause.

A strange juxtaposition—East and West—but not, as yet, if ever, a true mingling.

The Mendicant

THERE he stood in the doorway, ringing his little bell and waiting for the housewife or her husband to slide back the grated panels and to drop a few coins in his cup. Across his shoulder hung the gold brocaded band that is the emblem of the priests who serve the Buddha. He looked weary and jaded, this mendicant of an old, old Faith who was going thus from door to door to raise the funds so sorely needed to rebuild the temple that the flames had claimed.

It was not a prosperous district, but it had been all rebuilt after the Great Earthquake—all but the temple. The shops and homes were of new wood and roofed with tin; the temple courtyard still lay a barren waste. The bell tinkled on and on as the priest waited patiently, waited with the patience which he taught to others. No word was uttered. He was not there to plead his cause by word of mouth or to exhort. He merely swung the bell of bronze in patient supplication.

It will be, when rebuilt again, a most lovely temple, a temple reared by the tones of little bells.

The Inn

AS is customary, the master of the inn met us at the door with low bows and the indrawn breath of courtesy, while maids scuttered about in excitement, for this town of mid-Japan is not on the beaten track and it is seldom that the town, or the inn, plays the host to foreigners.

Further evidence of this is given at dinner, when it is discovered that there is not a bite of meat in the whole community of thirty thousand, not even a strip of bacon, only fish and eggs, chickens and vegetables and grain.

The boiling hot bath, without which no Japanese considers life complete, is prepared, and we are ushered to the bathroom by one of the maids, carrying a tiny Japanese towel over her arm. Even though the foreigner is a stranger to this coastal town some word of his curious habits and prejudices must have filtered in, for the maid does not remain to scrub our backs as she would have done a half-century or less ago had we chanced to lodge at the inn.

The simple, child-like curiosity characteristic of the Japanese, a curiosity in which no intentional rudeness is mingled, comes into play at dinner, when the whole staff of the hotel gathers about us as we sit on the floor eating, while they laugh gleefully at the clumsy handling of our chopsticks.

Afoot in Izu

"SHIN NEN O Medeto Gozaimasu!" which is translated as a "A Happy New Year to You," greeted us from every passing peasant girl or fisher boy as we four Americans tramped along the road that skirts the beautiful coast of the Izu Peninsula. The brilliant sunshine of the first morn of the year streamed down with a welcome warmth, high mountain ranges sheltering the coast of Sagami Bay from the more rigorous weather of the winter season. The blue waters of the bay were skipped here and there with a foaming whitecaps. The green-clad sides of the island known as Hatsushima lay close at hand, and farther out to sea the misty outlines of Oshima rose from the waters, a thin spiral of smoke curling from the ever-active volcano which marks that mountain-island's crest.

The road rose and dipped as it wandered along the broken coast line. Some times it touched the sea and again it soared up over cliffs of volcanic stone at the base of which the waves broke in foaming glory. A tiny hamlet here and a few scattered rice fields carved out of the steep slopes of the mountains brought the human note into this picture of loveliness, a note without which no Japanese considers the picture complete.

The whole of Japan was in holiday mood, for had not the New Year dawned and all was washed afresh, ready for the coming months? Pines and bamboo marked each gateway; straw rope and oranges and the other ancient symbols of the season were suspended over every door. The Sun Flag fluttered from tall poles of newly cut bamboo that were still green, and gay banners were strung along the masts of little fishing barques drawn up along the beach in idleness on this day of merry-making.

It was along this road, the Sea Road to Shimoda, that Townsend Harris had come up to Yedo in those days when America kindly but forcibly—and what American so fearful or so prejudiced as to say mistakenly?—insisted that Japan take its place among the nations of the world. Long before this first American envoy had passed this way the road was famous. Names that ring through the history of the Empire cling about its well-trod stones, and its beauties have been recorded by generation upon generation of poets and artists.

Modern times are having their way now, but less so than in many parts of Japan. At each end the ancient trail has given way to a well constructed motor road, but between them still lies a stretch that is now as it has been for centuries.

The four Americans seemed strangely out of place in these surroundings. In Tokyo, with its modern buildings and its curiously bewildering transition from the past to the present, they fitted well enough, but here one might have stepped back through several hundred years and be marching with a civilization that is vanishing.

Smiles and words of courteous greeting from the

peasant folk to those strangers showed that they were welcome. Much that is derogatory has been written of Japanese courtesy and it has often been asserted that it is purely formal, the result of long training that does not spring from the heart. It is impossible for the unbiased to live long in Japan, to move among its people, to get away from hotels and clubs and offices —especially offices—and out into the country without realizing the falseness of such charges. Not only by word and smile, but by action after action do the Japanese demonstrate the sincerity of their courtesy and desire to please the foreigner.

On this New Year's morn each was dressed in his best, and those whose means permitted it were wearing bright new kimono. The cheery greeting was flung broadcast with a wholesome heartiness that bespoke the well wishes prompting its utterance. "Shin nen O Medeto Gozaimasu!" If we paused to ask our way guides offered themselves gratis to go with us and to point it out at the more difficult spots.

From the rail head at Atami to the hot springs at Ito the way can not be lost, for this bit of the old Shimoda Kaido has been made into a modern motor road. It is a curving road of beauty, a road that in other lands would be exploited for the tourist but that in Japan is merely enjoyed for itself.

The Second Day

Beyond Ito the modern world is left behind and Old Japan is entered. It is not the Japan of the warrior samurai, but the Japan of simple peasant folk. True, the imprint of the feudal lord is visioned here and there, in the very construction of the road itself for that matter, but this is a land of farmers and burners of charcoal, of wood-cutters and of those who find their living in the sea.

The road, if road it can now be called, swings outward to the coast and again cuts inland over high mountain passes. It is paved in many places with huge stones, and the mountain climbs are made over rocky steps. Giant cryptomeria shelter the tea house found at the crest of each ascent, and thickets of bamboo are interspersed with forests of green pine trees. Where possible, rice fields have been hewed out or built up, but this land does not easily lend itself to cultivation by man.

A charcoal burner comes ambling by, seeming to be a figure from the stage, and guides us to a mountain village inn for lunch. Most of the village clusters round to see the foreigners, staring with good-natured curiosity and with no idea of rudeness.

As night falls we reach another village, this time a tiny spa by the seashore which has but two small inns. Both are filled to overflowing with their New Year guests, and the mistress of the inn is sore perplexed. Here are four Americans who have no place to sleep and she no shelter for them. What to do? Then three young clerks from Tokyo, guests at the inn, step forward. They have two rooms among them. They will all move into one room and give us the other. Another guest steps up and says he can do with one less coverlet that night. And so Japanese courtesy springs into action.

The Third Day

The next morning the ancient trail is resumed,

and it seems still more lovely. Coastal villages are passed through which are very much as they were centuries ago, save that a few Western products may be seen for sale in little shops along with the products of Japan. On over the mountains or along the coast winds the trail, until once more it turns into a motor road, a motor road that is building from the south to meet in time its companion coming from the north and so link the entire coast with modern transportation.

Italy, Switzerland, the Norse country—none can offer more of the beauty of Nature than does Japan, and of all Japan few places are as lovely as this eastern coast of Izu. The island-studded bay with its background of high mountains; the magnificent sweep of bay-indented shore; the tender delicacy of bamboo foliage and the more sombre toned needles of the pine; orange trees and trees of tea and the flowers of the wild camellia—even the plum is blossoming at New Year's tide in this sheltered spot.

The road sweeps down the mountains into Shimoda at last. The American is welcome in Shimoda, welcome as he is in few places in this world. The village has not forgotten its honor of being home to the first American envoy, who is still loved and honored throughout these islands. Now and again the American Ambassador to Tokyo comes to this spot to honor Townsend Harris and his work, and even the lowliest of his countrymen is taken to the hearts of those who dwell here.

The inn where the late Ambassador Bancroft slept still treasures this distinction, and some visiting foreigner has earned eternal gratitude by explaining to its mistress how to do several little things that add greatly to the comfort of the foreigner staying in a Japanese inn,

As we sit there, laughing and hungry while the sukiyaki cooks, willing to rest content after the tramp down the coast of the peninsula, there comes floating across the garden strains of music played by a strolling theatrical troupe with a foreign style band, and, curiously but appropriately enough in this spot, the tune is that of "Yankee Doodle."

Looking at Japan

IN the little town of Mito on Numazu Bay one seems to be detached and looking back at Japan. Across the blue waters that are skipped into whiteness by the wind rises a dark range of mountains, and towering behind them the snow-covered crests of the Southern Alps of Japan. To the right, framed by the peaks of two pine-clad islands, soaring above the world, ethereal and worshipful, floats the inverted fan of Fujisan, the white mantle of the winter season drooping from the peak far down the sweeping sides that are rhythmic as a symphony.

Victory!

THE sun, an hour old at least that August dawn, was veiled, obscured, made dimmer than the moon by thick, dense clouds. It glimmered faint and silver through the pall again and once again; then darkened in defeat. A hazy half-light like unto the weird aura of some ghostly realm before the earth was born prevailed on land and sea.

Between two distant pine-clad islands a sailboat drifted. It cut the world in twain, divided sea and sky, brought back into reality the horizon that had melted into nothingness. Close to the shore the creaking of long oars proclaimed that the dream world made by a deadened sun and deadening clouds was but a dream, that men still lived and moved and had their being.

Bound and enfeebled by the strangling clouds, the sun still struggled to prevail. Defeated in the heavens, it sought elsewhere to prove its right to rule. The new-found horizon, pricked into sensient sight now by the square-cut sail of the fisherman's boat and framed at each end by the dark green islands of the bay, became a gleaming silver line. The Lord of Day had found his vantage point.

Slowly but with timeless speed the silver streak that marked the boundary of two worlds was widening out into a broader band. The polish on the waters crept toward the shore; the whitening glow ascended till it reached the nether bank of clouds. The ghostly dream light of the lagging dawn grew clearer, more distinct, but still remained an eerie, mystic glimmer. The minutes passed, each one a victory for the warring sun.

There arose the call of fishers, loading their nets and making ready to set sail into the east, confident in the strength of the Lord of the Heavens. The song of a cicada broke the quiet stillness that lay on land and polished bay. A tiny breeze freshened the waters into a ripple that swept toward the beach, there to crash in spray which reached out to catch in pale reflection the silver of the far horizon and so bring the light to land. The light increased; gnarled pines and curved roofs of tile or thatch stood out in sharp relief. The clouds swirled in agony, knowing full well extinction was approaching them. The sun shot piercing beams into their midst, now striking through them at this point, again at that. Silver was fading, making way for the gold that was to come. The battle royal was in progress and its outcome was fore-ordained.

With a final surge still nearer to the zenith the giant orb rose above the clinging, entangling embrace of earth-loving clouds and poured in sudden splendor the full might of its great glory on the world. Hands and heads of simple Shinto fishermen were lifted toward the east to greet in reverence the coming of the light; the myriad-broken cloud bank drooped in remnants toward the surface of the water; the cry of the one cicada swelled into a triumphant chorus.

Day had come!

The Poems of Japan

> The swallow-flights of song that dip
> Their wings in tears, and skim away.

FROM one of the most musical and most unredeemably English of English poets comes this alien uta that curiously depicts so truly, both by definition and example, the delicate poems that the children of Japan have wrought throughout the centuries. The lonely pathos, the memory-stirring metaphor, the essential rhythm and the disregard of rhyme, the single, close-compressed idea that opens wide the vistas of enchantment to the dreaming soul: All of the chaste qualities of the thirty-one syllable uta of Japan are in these English words of Alfred Tennyson.

Poetry, as he knows it, is not a thing apart but a gossamer strand interwoven with the multitude of threads that make up the fabric of life to the Japanese. It has always been thus. Poems are the polychrome dragonflies darting about the shores of a lake, are drifting bits of thistledown, are tiny crystal balls in which the gazer sees dream-beauty as the truth, the very essence of existence.

Throughout the centuries the Mikado and his Court, the lords and ladies of the land, the warriors and statesmen, priest and artist and artisan, the common merchant and the peasant, all Japanese from the highest to the lowest have brushed off tiny bits of song as their hearts stirred them, and have gathered by some clear running stream or under the light of a full moon to hold poetry parties.

Each twelvemonth still, thousand upon thousand of the Japanese pay tribute to the glory of their Emperor and to his line in song. At New Year's time each subject of the August Mikado, no matter how humble or how great his rank, can lift his voice in rhythmic praise, can breathe devotion, loyalty and reverence through the wee poem he sends unto the Palace. From the huts of charcoal burners in the mountains, from the gaudy Western home of narikin, from winter villas on warm sheltered beaches and from thatched cottages that cluster close about drear rice fields come the poems to the Palace. The Emperor himself, the Heir Apparent and their nearest kindred join in the feast of song with which the coming of the year is welcomed to the Isles of Sunrise.

From out the myriad poems that are woven around the subject of Imperial designation a few are chosen to be honored by a ceremonial reading in the presence of the Court and of a few distinguished guests. In English they sound strange, unfinished, seem but broken bits of poetry, like the single petal of a wild rose torn from its delicate companion petals and the heart of gold whence it sprang. Hark back to Tennyson's couplet, to the uta of an Englishman, in reading the poems of Japan and recall the words of still another son of Albion who dwelt long in Nippon, of W. G. Aston, from whom I here borrow.

"* * * * they seem to me like a rosary of beautiful beads, lustrous and dark, starry and somber, clear as the autumn moon or mysterious as an ancient forest. Within the narrow limits of the uta, as in that other serious convention, the tsuba, or sword-guard, the Japanese creative faculty contrives to enshrine all that it holds dear and in reverence—all that it fears, too, thereby stilling the tremor of the heart awhile."

The very naming of the subject for the New Year poems is itself an uta without form. "Before the Shrine at Dawn" one season inspired the now Empress Dowager to write:

> The walls of the Great Shrine at Ise
> Seen at dawn
> Are clean,
> Reminding one of the Cave of Heaven
> Of which legends tell.

"The Rising Sun on the Waves" was the theme the following year, and then there came "Clouds on the Mountain at Daybreak," and Her Imperial Majesty wrote:

> With a purified mind at daybreak I look up
> At the white clouds on Mount Asakuma

There was one New Year's season when the tragedy of the Great Earthquake lay close behind but was redeemed by the hope of the future, and "The Dawn of the New Year" was the subject chosen.

As the marriage of the Prince Regent, now the Emperor, and Princess Nagako Kuni approached it was the thought running through many of the uta, and in none other was it better expressed than in the poem of the Princess' mother:

> Underneath the spreading arms of a pine tree
> In the garden of the palace
> A couple of young cranes
> Raise a permanent chorus of joy.

"The Mountain Crest Against the Sky" is an imperfect rendering into English of the thought embodied in the poems one year. There was less of that haunting melancholy sadness than usual, but the sanctified spirit of the dedication of the soul was there, the spirit that had been so well expressed several years previously in these two uta by Baroness Kujo and Akiko Yosano:

> The calm of this moment
> Is very precious,
> There is no sound in heaven or earth,
> And I am alone with the moon.

> As the smoke of the incense in my porcelain burner
> Floats upward
> On this spring day of mine,
> My room is like a great temple
> And my heart serene.

Since the ninth century the poems of the Imperial Family have been read three times and then chanted by Court musicians. The uta of the Empress Dowager on the Mountain Crest, of the Emperor and of his Empress are:

> Splendidly clad in snow white,
> Mount Fuji reigns supreme
> Over the low surrounding hills

Which melt into the atmosphere
Blending with the azure of the sky.

May as manly be our reign
As that towering height
Of splendid Mount Tateyama.

Humbly I bowed,
Facing east to meet
That solemn first ray of the New Year's sun;
Turning, I met
The great mountain of Fuji
Towering high into sky.

And then, to bind closer the poetic thought of the East and West, there are these four bits of beauty snatched from out the longer poems of Richard Jeffries, of John Webster, of Walt Whiteman and of William Morris, which, standing by themselves, might well be hokku or uta of Japan:

When the crescent of the new moon shone,
All the old thoughts were renewed.

My soul, like to a ship in a black storm,
Is driven, I know not whither.

A horn sounding through the tangle of the forest,
And the dying echoes.

Friendly the sun, the bright flowers and the grass
Seemed after the dark wood.

The Moon of March

IT was the full moon of mid-March that drew me forth. The white tracery of the virgin plum, first of all the blossoming trees of Japan to brave the snows, gleamed wanly in the moonlight. The breath of Spring was in the soft night air, and what appeal had lights and laughter and the talk of men against the magic of the night?

It was the full moon that drew me forth from out the overlighted house, and it was its dimly brilliant beams that lured me on, on through streets thick-crowded from house line to house line, filled with men bargaining for their daily rice, filled with weary women resting for a moment and forgetting toil, filled with gay children who knew no other playground than the public way but who know happiness.

Here a man-made light glowed dully through an opaque shoji of milk-white rice paper; there the cruel glare of this modern age struck through thin glass to reveal in stark brutality the revel and the babel and confusion that men make for themselves; above, the gentle moon slipped half behind a billowy black cloud, lacquering with an aura of pale gold the darkening sky.

Wild laughter and still wilder shouts came from the curtained entrances of cheap cafes that have sprung up all over Tokyo. A breath of hot, damp, cloying air swept from a public bath house as the door slid noisily in its grooves and a man, red as the rambler rose of June, stepped out. Life, drab and joyous, unkempt and puritanical, throbbed all about, and there was scant space for the quiescent glory of the overhanging moon.

Through streets of noise and smells, through alleys of strange sights, quiet but more insistent than the call of men came the enchantment of the mid-March moon.

An arching bridge of stone across a semi-stagnant moat gave passage to rough-hewn steps winding upward to the heights above. Surely the moon would be there, the full moon of mid-March, the moon that filled with magic the warm night in promise of the Spring.

A Shinto shrine, its dull red paint and ornate carvings telling the tale of the day when two religions were as one, stood silent and deserted on the mount that reared itself above all housetops in the middle of the sprawling city. The well-trod earth, beaten smooth and grassless by a thousand, thousand feet, yielded with a spongey restfulness. Tall trees, their straight trunks towering like the pillars of a mighty temple, their branches tinged with just the tiniest of buds, reared gaunt and black, black as the shadow that they cast. A single taper fluttered toward its death within a votary stone lantern, and the lingering scent of incense came drifting through the dark, so faint and so ethereal that it seemed the sweet breath of the moonbeams filtering through the night.

Long-drawn, melodious and quaveringly poignant rose the call of the hot noodle man, making his night-ly rounds on the streets below. A distant strain of jazz, ground out on some machine, broke for a moment as the door of a cafe swung open and then shut again. The breeze stirred the branches and they grated, grated, the bare limbs refusing to give out the softer murmur that the leaves of summer bring.

The city lay below, its noise and clamour, gaiety and bitterness, a distant thing. Here, trees and the beaten earth, height and the inspiration of the heights, were close at hand. Above—the moon!

It was the full moon of mid-March. The pale blossoms of the plum responded to its call. The earth, and all earth's creatures, felt it. The strange melodies of a strange race came echoing through the night. Lights and dark shadows, joy and the baser heart throbs of humanity, were so far, so very far away, and yet, so unmistakably close and present. Witchery and dreams, the beauty for which the soul reaches and can grasp if it but forget the reaching, were living things.

Spring was being born that night, and one sensed the rustling movements of the Old Man of the Moonlight as he flitted here and there, tying together with his unseen, silken cord of crimson the hearts and souls and tiny bodies of the new-born baby boys and baby girls destined for each other when their lives should flower.

The World Awakens

Clang — clang — clang — !
LIKE the ringing of the blacksmith's anvil, only wider spaced, the tones of the Buddhist bell float upward through the opened shoji to steal into the sleeper and to tell him that the sun is lifting from the blue Pacific to shine once more on the Isles of Japan.

Clang — clang — clang — steadily but not in a monotonous way the strokes on metal continue. The twittering of awakened sparrows blends with the sonorous notes of the bronze bell that hangs near the gold Buddha on the floor below. The coolness of the dawn steals through the palms and pines, bamboo and maple trees. Out on the narrow public street there rises the clear call blown from a conch as the white-clad, bare brown-legged seller of fish goes from door to door, bearing his double burden in great round wooden baskets swinging from the pole he shifts from shoulder to shoulder.

Clang—clang—clang—. Clack—clack—clack—clack—. A new note has joined the full tones of the bell, for another worshipper or perhaps a young priest in training has picked up the wooden blocks like castanets and is clapping them together that the constant repetition of their sound may in some small way convey the idea of eternity, of Nirvana.

The blue-gray light turns to pink; to gold. The

clang of small bronze bell and clack of wooden blocks die away. In turn, there sounds the deep-toned voice of some ancient bell of Korea, too mighty to hang within the temple walls, its mellow boom announcing that the day has come. "Namu Amida Butsu!" The murmured, mumbled words of faith are meant for the God of India brought to this land so long ago to hear and harken to. The Buddhist world awakes and starts its day of toil with prayer.

A Happy Land

ON those days when it is not too misty, or when soft clouds of rain do not enfold Tokyo, or when the dust does not swirl up from the city's streets, if one look out across the waters of Tokyo Bay toward the east the ridges of blue mountains will be perceived floating between earth and sky. They are the mountains that march down the Boshu Peninsula, and among the highest of them is Kano-zan.

The peninsula of Boshu is a land unto itself. It is a smiling land, prosperous and contented. It is near to the modern city of Tokyo, but it is not of the city. Among its shrines and temples are a few which go back to the very dawn of history. It was, so they who should know tell me, once an island itself, and insular it remains in thought and outlook as the tide of Westernism sweeps over the ports and cities of Japan.

Boshu has not kept pace with the Japan that we of the cities know, but the trite phrase, "a bit of Old Japan," is ashes in the mouth when speaking of Boshu. It is much as it was when the Tokugawa ruled with iron hand in ancient Yedo, and much as it must have been in the days even before the might of that powerful family. And yet, "a bit of Old Japan" conjures up an utterly false image of the land of its people.

There are no ghostly samurai riding in armour such

as one feels at Sekigahara or about the broken walls of the Osaka Keep. There is not the pageantry of a daimyo's train moving along the Tokaido beneath dignified cryptomeria. There is not the primaeval simplicity of Yamada-Ise nor the mellowed grandeur and beneficence of the temple roofs of Kyoto. But, I wonder, is there not more perhaps of Old Japan in Boshu today than in most of the story books we read which tell of battles and Bushido, of cherry blossom poems and of Genji the Shining One? For Boshu is a peasant land.

Along its lovely seacoast fishermen set out each clear day and on nights when the moon shines brightly, simple fisherfolk intent on their catch and ready to make merry when the nets are full in the way in which all simple folk make merry. In its fertile valleys the father, the wife and the son all toil in the muck of rice field or of garden patch that Tokyo may eat. Charcoal burners and woodcutters dwell among its mountains, and honest physical labor is accepted without question and without regret as part of life by all.

It is not a land of grandeur, but it is a land of happiness. Its coastline is mostly low and unimpressive but its waters teem with fish. Its valleys are now narrow, now wide, but all are planted with life-giving grain or vegetables. Even its mountains are not high, yet they are wild and primitive in a way that the tourist haunts of the Hakone and near Nikko know not.

Its people live and work and die, take their pleasure and their sadness aloof from the turmoil and raucous sounds of the transitional stage through which so much of Japan is going. They live much as did their fathers, and they think much as did those who dwelt there a hundred years and more ago. The shrine festival still triumphs over the motion picture show, and the moon is still more important than Pope Gregory in determining what day it is.

Modern civilization has, of course, sent out its tentacles to Boshu and they seem to be welcomed there as elsewhere. Motor bus services thread the narrow roadways of the peninsula; glass has replaced rice paper in many a shop front; beer, as well as sake, has become a universal beverage. The lads who go out from the fishing hamlets or from the handkerchief-farms to serve with the Colors return with new fangled ideas and act as a powerful medium in standardizing this country, adjacent to and yet so isolated from that curious mixture we call Tokyo.

This survival of the past, this remnant of rural Japan when Japan was a world unto itself, is destined to fall in step in time, but until that time comes it has something precious to offer him who will but make the effort to partake of it.

I can not but wonder whether Boshu as it is, this peninsula of fisherfolk and peasants, is not more truly representative of Old Japan than are the tales of warriors and of the pomp of the Tokugawa Court. Was not the real heart of Japan to be found among its farmers and its workers rather than among its samurai? Was it not here that the glory of Dai Nihon found its basis? And if so then, is it not just as true today? Japan has changed—but not that much.

The blue ridge of Kano-zan calls and beckons across the waters of Tokyo Bay to the dwellers in that dusty city. The city may be left behind and a simple Arcady entered if one but will.

Out from the Marunouchi district with its modern buildings and its millions grubbing for a living and a competence, out through the factory district and the slums that lie beyond the Sumida River, on out to where the road swings back to the shores of Tokyo Bay and the bay lies to the west instead of to the south and east runs the road to Kano-zan.

The breeze freshens and is caught by the square-cut sails of fishing junks. Army post after army post rolls by and the road is filled with the khaki-clad conscripts who have replaced the two-sworded aristocrats of other days. Garrisons dot this region almost as thickly as do villages. An aerodrome for flying boats stands next the shelving beach. Is it that Japan needs thus to be so well protected? Or is that some place in an overcrowded Empire must be found to pack her hordes of soldiers. Dogs bark and children call a greeting. The country becomes more and more rural, less and less indicative of a densely peopled nation, and at last the town of Chiba flashes into view.

Chiba, the ugly capital of Chiba Prefecture, is not quite so ugly in its holiday attire for the summertide of Tokyoites seeking refuge and recreation along its beach. For a mile or more summer stalls of cut bamboo and matting have been erected, reared on stilts that they may be above high tide. Gay banners of red and blue and white are strung across their low eaves, proclaiming the coolness of ice cream or the nutriment of peanuts or the rare delicacy of shell fish.

The road curves southward and Tokyo Bay now lies to the west. The hill tops loom ahead, the hills that give the impression of mountains rising from the coastal plain. It is a prosperous land, this farming-fishing country, that nestles on the inner shore of shallow Tokyo Bay. The homes along the wayside are well kept and neat. Spacious kitchens and the clucking of many chickens bear their testimony. Gardens of flowers and smoothly clipped hedges are not found where the daily struggle barely brings sufficient rice for the daily meal.

On down the gentle shores to Kisarazu and then inland for nine miles goes the road. Slight hills and dales are crossed and the fields rise in terraces toward the crests. This is a smiling valley, a valley where the fields and trees and hills seem to join with the peasants in their greeting to the strangers fleeing from the city's dust and grime. Farms and bamboo groves flash by as the road winds up the valley to the base of Kano-zan. The green greenness of young rice tones into the more sombre shades of the trees and bamboo grass on the hillsides. The fields are filled with workers bending low to transplant the tender rice shoots from one field, into another, plodding laboriously through the deep muck behind a primitive plough drawn by a single ox, straightening or pausing in their work to smile a welcome to the passer-by. Millions of young frogs raise their chorus, and wild flowers embroider the low hills that shut in the peaceful valley.

There are three trails which lead up Kano-zan. One of them has now been made into a motor road. Another is an easy ascent and is lovely, but in a pastoral way. The third is steep and sandy, is difficult to climb, but it is this third which rewards the climber with a beauty that is breath-taking.

Straight up that path goes, straight up unto the highest peak in all the district. It winds but little, steep as a ladder, choked with sand, it has been trod by innumerable feet through the long centuries since first Yamato Takeru-no-Mikoto slew a demon there, since the day when Prince Shotoku founded the Buddhist temple-monastery that still survives, since the day when that great artist-artisan, Hidari Jingoro, carved with his left hand the gateway to that temple.

Up, up it goes; and then along the level for a space while the eye sweeps out over the magnificent valley that is ever falling farther away. Through tunnels of trees and great masses of wild honeysuckle it climbs until the crest is reached, and then a panorama is beheld which can never be erased from memory.

Kuju-ku Tani, the Ninety-Nine Valleys, spread their serrated greenness far below. Sharp, irregular ridges stretch in all directions and at all angles, crossing and crisscrossing, forming a spectacle like a giant relief map, green-clad and lovely. From their depths the song of nightingales and their kindred of the air arises, filling, so it seems, the whole universe with their chorus of sweet music.

The path has now widened out and is lined with mountain cherry trees as it approaches the little village. Houses are thatched with straw and are of the simplest construction. Children play in the single street and it seems that Marunouchi must be a thousand, thousand miles away. A great red temple with an elaborately and beautifully carved gateway stands at the head of some crude steps, dividing the village in twain. It is a prosperous temple, for this is a prosperous district and the people still are pious in the Japanese sense of that term. And why should it not be well kept up? In it dwells the spirit of Yamato Takeru-no-Mikoto, one of the eighty children of the Emperor Keiko, he who first subdued the barbarians of Eastern Japan and brought this wild land under the sway of the August Mikado.

On past the temple lies the inn, the Inn of Seven Circles. It, too, is primitive, without luxuries, but clean. Its darkened timbers tell its age, and the courtesy of its few attendants bespeaks their welcome to the stranger.

Through the entrance way one walks and then, without previous warning, there bursts upon one the most magnificent view in all this part of Japan.

The mountain falls away below the inn. To the far left the tip and the whole length of the Izu Peninsula is seen gleaming in the sunlight, the crest of the Amagi Mountains still snow-capped. To the far right rise the mountains about Nikko, and lonely Tsukuba-san. Between them in the background are the Hakone and the Chichibu ranges, and behind, towering over all in its sublimity, floats the perfect cone of flawless Fujisan.

Below lie the waters of all of Tokyo Bay. The eye sweeps from its entrance up the far coast to Yokosuka and then out to Yokohama. Tsurumi, Kawasaki and Omori are ranged in line and then the whole of sprawling Tokyo presents itself for this memory-searing view. Even the town of Chiba to the right is seen.

The sun drops rapidly and the shadows darken

on the bay below. Izu Peninsula begins to dim; the Nikko Mountains soon will fade from sight. The August Mountain claims tribute from the departing sun glowing first like purest gold, only to change to ruby crimson before it, too, is absorbed into the darkening night.

Light-houses at the entrance to the bay and on the islands that lie beyond begin to twinkle their messages of safety. Slowly, one by one at first and then all in a blaze, the cities and the towns along the bay shore burst into golden stars. From Yokosuka to Chiba the bay front is thus dotted with the shining stars of men, while above the sky is pricked out with its points of brilliancy as the Lady Moon sails silently, disdainfully, laughing perhaps, from her superior heights at man's attempt thus to raise himself so far above the world which he has builded.

A First Principle.

THE single blossom of a morning glory, deep blue and streaked with crimson, poised on the moist soft breeze of a summer's dawn that swept into the simple hut to give tribute before the tokonoma and its treasure, greeted the eyes of the Taiko, the first lord of all Japan. The rest of the once glorious garden he had come to see lay bare, a vast expanse of whitened gravel.

Anger reddened the great man's cheeks.

And then he heard the words of Rikyu, master of the cha-no-yu, the low tones of the artist guiding the governor in the way of art. The anger paled to shame, but that, too, vanished.

The single bloom of a morning glory had been made perfect by desolating a garden, and in that white garden with its one gleam of pulsing, living beauty lay the whole world of Japanese aestheticism and art.

Pioneers of Empire

HIGH pitched and quavering, the words of the pioneer on the fringe of Empire are thrown back by the lonely banks of the broad Yalu River to the sun-bronzed men on rafts of logs floating down the stream, flung back to those from whose throats they come.

> Hakutozan, ukiyo hanarete sodatta watashi,
> Imawa kirarete ikadabune, yoisho,
> Fuchini tadayoi yo ano seni sekare yo,
> Nagare mata nagarete Shingishu, choi, choi.

("O, Mount Hakuto, upon whose slopes I grew, far removed from this world of vicissitudes! Now I am cut down and fashioned into a raft; now I drift on to this bank; now I am hurried over this shallow as I am borne down stream. On I go drifting until I reach Shingishu.")

It is the tree itself that is speaking, the magnificent pine or birch that has been felled in the mighty forests where Korea and Manchuria touch. The words come from the lips, and from the heart, of the son of Dai Nippon who has put his homeland behind him and has struck out into an ancient land that is still new and strange to most the world. Into the cold mountains and forests of Northern Korea he has gone in search of fortune, but he has carried with him into this rude wilderness as his dearest treasure the memories of that more gentle way of living which he knew at home.

Jiuta—place songs—are the popular music of Japan. Folk songs, they might be called, but no ballad can really claim that title until it has proved its enduring worth by being flung from lip to lip down through long years. There are jiuta of other centuries which are still sung to the twang of geisha's samisen, or whistled by the schoolboys of the cities. Others are quite new. They are not "written" as are the songs heard in Western lands. The jiuta, although it may be modern, is always the voice, of the folk living and working and loving in the locality whose tale it tells. Other verses may be added later when the song creeps into the partly Westernized ports and cities of the Empire, but these additions do not carry the flavor of the original.

Of all the jiuta to be heard in Japan today, those that have arisen from the hearts of the pioneers on the borders of the Empire are most appealing. From the banks of the far-flung Yalu their call has echoed to the homeland, and the homeland has listened and echoed it back.

> Chosen to Shina no sakai no ano Oryokko,
> Kakeshi tekkyo wa arya toyo-ichi, yoisho;
> Juji ni hirakeba yo ano maho kataho yo,
> Yukiko janku no nigiwashisa choi, choi.

("The Yalu River that divides Korea from China—great is its steel bridge, the greatest in the Orient; behold! Through the frame it makes as it swings across the river the countless junks gliding under, their sails of many shapes on the way of peaceful prosperity.")

The glory of Japan is not forgot by her son who wanders into the far corners, and all Japan is proud of the great bridge of metal that spans the Yalu at Antung and Shingishu, on the border of Manchuria. To the wood cutters, the lumbermen and the raft hands who pass beneath it, the bridge must seem a vital symbol of the might of their homeland, a seal that has been placed on the hills and waters of Korea to show that they are now part of Japan. Even the naked steel trusses of a railway bridge can become a thing of beauty when painted with the word pictures of song. This song, the "Oryokko Bushi," for Oryokko is the Japanese reading of the Chinese characters which mean Yalu, is the most popular of all such in Japan.

Japan's Gift

FRAMED by the lines of the opened shoji, the pink-petalled blossom of a curiously twisted plum tree that heralds the spring felt the soft touch of falling flakes of snow as the gray light came with the dawn of the day that was neither spring nor winter. The white flakes melted into nothingness as they touched the dark brown ground, damp from the rains of the day before. They lingered in more friendly spirit on the sword-like leaves of the bamboo and made a tiny drift of whiteness in the curves of the old stone lanterns. The Higan, when the souls of the departed cross over the River of Heaven and when winter passes into spring, is almost here. The blossoms of the plum tree have already touched with color the earth that the drear winter season had grayed into a toneless, passionless monotony. Soft winds from out the south have borne the gentle warming rains from adown the Pacific and the full moon of March has passed its zenith. The call of spring is in the air and its whispering voice echoes in the heart. With each dawn there comes a chorus of song from the birds that have winged their way back from the southern isles to joy once more in the glory of the summer of a more northern land.

The winter has come and almost gone, the winter is dying, but this season the winter failed to bring its gift of beauty, failed to pay its tribute of the snow that alone entitles it to visit earth. As if fearful that this neglect would bring retribution, the departing coldness paused for a second in its flight to scatter its own white crystal blossoms in rivalry to the flowers of the plum and to the still unopened buds of other trees and shrubs that will make glad the months that lie so close ahead.

The Snow and the Blossoms, the Rain and the Moon: Here is the poetry of Old Japan; here is the inspiration of the wood block artists; here is the gift of Nature that man seeks to keep with him forever by imprisoning it in the words and notes of songs, in the colors and the clear-cut lines of the ukiyoye.

There are not four seasons in Japan that are known as winter and spring, summer and the autumn-tide. There are not the times of cold and heat. There are not four sets of three months each. These are things of the calendar, of science, of practical matter-of-fact "getting things done." With such affairs the symbolical culture of Old Japan had naught to do. There are, rather, the Time of Snow and the Time of Blossoms; the Time of Rain and the Time of the Moon.

He who would know and understand Japan must attune himself to this symbolism that has been wrought out through centuries of aesthetic worship of the beautiful. It is Japan's great gift to the world, a gift at which the Japan of today is far too prone to scoff, although in the heart of hearts there must still be treasured the devotion to beauty that is the nation's heritage. In this modern world other values weigh for more. The emphasis has been placed elsewhere. And Japan, examining itself, discovers lack of gifts that the West has for the world, becoms proudly, foolishly heartsick, turns with determination to mechanics, science, warfare, practicality—most of which it sorely needs—but in the turning loses all sense of proportion and so undervalues its own gift of sheer symbolical aestheticism which we the world at large need quite as much.

Japan seeks to complete itself, seeks the compliment to its own gift that the West possesses, but it courts the great danger of losing what it has. May it not be that the West, too, may see the wisdom of seeking completement from the Eastern people?

When the snow falls in Japan there is no time for such introspection or for seeking answers to the puzzles that confront us. When the falling snow is greeted by the blossoms of the virgin plum aestheticism triumphs. The brief snatches of suggestion that are Basho's poems, the small square of paper that bears the echoed imprint of the brush of Hiroshige—these are the things that live as the great white flakes settle on the curved roofs of red lacquered temples, as they are absorbed in the embrace of the waters of the moat that are for them Nirvana, as they lie in rivalry to the fallen petals of the plums on the dark ground that the young year has not yet pierced with its green spears that will be destined to quick triumph.

In the crowded walks and pleasure places of Asakusa the snow is greeted with rejoicing by the youth of Japan. Their skirts tucked high to reveal gay petticoats beneath and with umbrellas of oiled paper held aslant, the maids and matrons who trip along on high stormy weather geta have indeed stepped from the frame that holds some rare print of a century and more ago. As the slowly deepening whiteness blankets the grounds of the shrine that is given over to the worship of the Emperor Meiji, the dark green of the pines and cryptomeria seems even darker and the breath of the primaeval, of the days when Jimmu Tenno roamed the forests and the mountains and the narrow strip of coastal plain, the mystic atmosphere of the days when first the Gods reclaimed the Eight Great Islands hovers near at hand.

The Time of Blossoms and the Time of Snow are met in one. Japan's gift of aesthetic symbolism is offered freely for the taking. To some it is a gift indeed; there are others who can not forget, even when it snows or when the blossoms blow, that life is "practical," who prefer half-living all the time to achieving completeness now and then.

Nihon no Koe

As the darkness falls, the drabness and the ugly, plain monotony of the capital of Japan yield to the soft embrace of less than semi-light. Lines that by day are sharp, severe, foreboding, dominating all, meld into the background of the scented voice-redundant night.

The moon sweeps up from the black waves of the Pacific, climbing slow and yet more slowly toward the vault of the great vast arch of Heaven. Thick clouds that must be milky white are touched by the moon's beams to glow like yet unlike unburnished silver.

The glance turns cityward, turns toward the over-Westernized district filled with tall buildings made of stone and brick, of steel and concrete. The moon is not the sovereign there, for the reflected glare of many bulbs of man-made light pulses like dull gold, rather than like silver, against the canopy of clouds.

Overhead the beauty of the night; here to the right and left, before, behind and all about, the wonder of an ugliness redeemed by darkness, scarcely given visibility by the moon and by more artificial brightness.

Shops are closed, barred tight by flimsy wooden screens against the air. A paper shoji, cut into small rectangles by cross-bracing strips, stands out alone amidst the darkness that surrounds it. The house is shapeless, formless, utterly invisible save for this checked rectangle of glowing opalescent light. A breeze from out the south stirs to whispering the mystery-laden branches of a pine, and for a moment the delicate clustered needles are silhouetted against the paper window-pane. A fleeting moment for the eyes; for the memory as long as life endures.

As if to match this seen symbolism of the strange fascination that Japan can exercise there rises on the almost tangible night air the haunting, mournful notes of a shakuhachi. The flute of pathos, breathed into by unknown lips, fingered by unseen hands, rises, ebbs and dies almost to nothingness. It, too, is of the night, mistily vapourous, compelling in its poignancy, as fleeting and as enduring as the slender pine branch pricked into life for a moment by the lighted background of the shoji.

To show that this is present-day Japan, to drag the dreamer back into reality, the door of a cafe swings wide. A brutal glare of yellow light streams out; the mechanism of the radio drowns out with its blatant, strident, harsh, metallic tones the tender wavering notes of the distant flute.

Mystery returns as the cafe is left behind.

Flickering candle flames before the altar of the Buddha enshrined in a tiny wayside temple dance through the door and gateway that the worshipper has left adjar. The steady tapping of a temple drum, man's feeble effort to create eternity, forms a slow undertone for the mumbled words of two young priests as they chant a mass for the repose of the soul of one who has crossed over the River of Heaven. Consolation and heart's ease can be procured for a handful of cash, if the heart be filled with faith.

Two young apprentices, the arm of one thrown lightly over the shoulders of his companion, stroll down the dim and narrow street, their faces and their half-clothed bodies warm and ruddy from the bath. Their laughter mingles with the other voices of the night.

A serving girl, weary and listlessly drooping, steps from the kitchen, glances skyward toward the moon and a smile of happiness flutters over her lips.

His bell ringing sharp and clear, a lad in workman's garments darts past on a bicycle, guiding with one hand while on the other is poised a tray laden with food that has been ordered from some nearby restaurant.

From behind the closed shoji of an upper storey comes the loud laughter of a merry-making group. The twanging of the samisen and the falsetto voice of geisha raised in song float out. There is heard the rhythm peculiar to festival music and the clapping of many hands in unison.

An automobile, modern convenience of the modern day, swings around a corner and its great headlights banish the shadows that have been so filled with eerie charm. The wide tires crush the gravel with a crunching sound and the electric horn flashes out to silence all the other voices for an instant.

Nihon no koe is a changing voice. One moment

there may be heard, the lingering notes of a too-rapidly forgotten past. The shakuhachi sounds; a badly played tune from out the West on radio, gramophone, piano demands attention. The rhythmic clatter of swift-running geta on stepping stones is followed by the blast of a klaxon. A kimono-clad geisha, hair piled high in ancient style, chatters gaily with her haikara escort proudly garbed in trousers, coat and leather shoes.

Of what use to protest? But regrets can not be denied.

My Lord of Sendai

MY Lord of Sendai, Date Masamune, he who aspired to the Shogun's power and dared dispatch a fragile barque from Nippon's shores unto the Pope at Rome and to the King of Spain in search of an alliance, sits enthroned behind an altar of the Buddhist fane where pilgrims bow in visiting Matsushima.

The giant cryptomeria of Japan shadow with their branches the stone path that leads unto the temple which has seen eleven centuries go by. The cliff of soft sandstone that lies upon one side of this avenue of stately trees is cut and carved by many score of caves. When Zuigan-ji was in the first flush of its glory the shaven followers of the Buddha dwelt in these caves. A thousand years ago, each had his niche in truth; some high, some low; all small.

The years have darkened or obliterated the tool marks that once cut away the rock. The years have softened rough outlines and have claimed their toll, breaking off great overhanging ledges which lie prone upon the ground. Wind and the rain, the freezing of the winter season and the heat of summertime, have slowly, quietly, resistlessly proclaimed their mastery over man. An image of the Buddha cut in bas-relief is little more than a mere shapeless outline now. Crumb by crumb the brown sandstone has been worn away, has yielded to decay and change.

The sombre teachings of the great religion born in India and creeping northward to Japan are here depicted in their fullness. Impermanence and transitoriness, the inevability of fate, the shadows that to the living in their little lifetime seem the substance—the solid rock itself is forced to yield its individuality as the centuries pass by, merging again into the soil, the air, the water, into elements that know naught of units but only unity.

These priests of long ago, mumbling their prayers, counting their rosaries, spinning the bronze or stone prayer-wheels, seeking and searching in their hearts for light, disciplining their desires and passions, striving not to strive or seek to strive but to recognize impermanence and so sink into an eternal non-existence for the individual—how much more eloquent is the sermon preached in silence by these age-worn caves of stone than any words they ever uttered!

The Lord of Sendai, Date Masamune, sits enthroned behind the alter of their temple.

Three hundred years ago he lived and dreamed his dreams and wrought his acts. Great acts they were, the daring of a valliant spirit not content to spend a lifetime dreaming. A warrior of Old Japan, a statesman of a troubled Empire, an ambitious diplomat he was, who struck out into the unknown with a courage that demands respect and admiration.

From the shores of these Eastern Islands he sent forth his tried and true retainer, voyaging across the broad Pacific, onward to the Tiber. What message may have been conveyed, how high the Lord of Sendai's great ambition may have soared, remain unknown.

No alliance with the Holy Father or the King of Spain ensued; Date Masamune died as he had lived, a feudatory of his liege the Tokugawa.

The Lord of Sendai sits enthroned. The years have passed, and with their passing may have dimmed, somewhat, the lustre of his name, but oblivion, nonexistence, lack of individuality are not for such as he.

In the fading glory of the temple that looks out across the waters to the pine-clad isles of Matsushima, the sons of Japan still make obeisance to the image and the spirit of the warrior.

Green bamboo and brilliant peacocks painted by the masters of the Kano School on golden silk for the expected visit of an Emperor have faded also with the passing centuries. Quaint figures passing up and down the gilded screens no longer flaunt their robes of crimson but have dimmed and darkened, have become shibui. The wood carving of the great Left-Handed Jingoro completes this Chamber of State.

Date Masamune, man of action, in the preparation of that room reveals his soul. Lord of a Northern Province, far from the Court at Kyoto with its sacred, deep-secluded Emperor, he prepared magnificently for the coming of that Emperor. Even the castle-palace of his Shogun-master in Old Yedo never knew the presence of the only man to whom the Shogun knelt. Date Masamune brought to the shores of Matsushima the master-artists, master-craftsmen of Japan, there to create a room of loveliness for the reception of the August Mikado. What dreams the warrior-statesman must have dreamed! What thoughts, ambitions must have stirred within him as he served the Tokugawa but prepared to bring about the realization of his dream of power!

The Lord of Sendai was a man of action. From the shores of his northern fief he sent forth an embassy to Rome and to Madrid. On those shores he made ready for the coming of the Emperor and his own succession to the Shogunate. He died—his dream unrealized.

Crumbling caves of weather beaten stone line the courtyards of the temple, caves of crumbling stone that tell of change, decay, impermanence. In that temple sits enthroned the Lord of Sendai, Date Masamune. Those thousand priests of a thousand years ago who sought self-extinction have attained it. Year by year their retreats of solid stone melt into nothingness. There is change, decay, impermanence—the eternity of non-existence.

Date Masamune, Lord of Sendai, he who dreamed and dared to act, he who broke the chains of custom, who sought aid from out of Christendom, but so unavailingly, sits enthroned as pilgrims bow in homage to his image and his spirit.

Life continuing, hero of the present, Date Masamune and his worshippers mock the crumbling caves of stone that preach the alien doctrine.

The Western Weavers

WE, aliens in a strange land, the Western weavers who are making a home in the East, fret and worry and complain of our surroundings; and are contented. We talk of the things which we find here, and we talk of the things which the East lacks.

There is life and death and work; love and marriage and giving in marriage and birth. There is food to eat and clothes for a shelter by day and a house for shelter by night. The big things are here just as truly as in the West, the great broad strands of the warp that stretch along the loom of life. The difference lies in the woof, the shading of the silk or cotton or linen threads which we weave back and forth across the warp that remains as it has been since the world began and as it is in all countries, all centuries.

So trite has become the statement "it is the little things that count" that we give a half-apologetic smile when we murmur it now. But the statement has become trite because it is true. The manner in which any saying becomes trite is by frequent repetition, and, scandal mongers to the contrary, it is only the true which is given such constant repetition.

It is the little things that count, but they count only as they fill out and complete the larger things.

The little thread of gold lying on the closet shelf

or thrown carelessly on the floor has no power to move and stir us, to bring us pleasure. It is only when that golden thread is taken by the weaver and drawn skilfully back and forth, over and under, the warp that it shapes itself into a pattern of loveliness. It is then it counts.

The warp of life in Japan is the same as in the West. The threads of the woof are somewhat different. Some are strange and fantastic, blending the pattern of the Orient in our lives.

Others are drab and dull. They serve to set off the beautiful, but the handling of them is far from beautiful, not can philosophers make it so. There is as little joy in filling in the background as there is in washing dishes or running errandes.

But these are two of threads that we Westerners do not have in the Far East, two of the little things that count. We do not have to wash our own dishes and the chit book is always handy. True, the telephone, which is the chit book of the West, is neither handy nor cheap. Certainly the servants, their comparative plentitude and cheapness and their efficiency, are bright threads for our looms. They are not golden threads, but they are at least blue or green or red. We grumble at them and about them, yes; but when the time comes to go home we would give much to take them with us; and to keep them as they are if we did.

There is one bright thread of the West that handicaps many of us in our Far Eastern weaving—the theatre. We have the brilliant color of the Japanese theatre, but it is too weird and too gorgeous to weave into the pattern often, lest its very strangeness disturb the even and regular design. Here and there is one who has mastered its handling and who is able to weave it into beautiful shapes that add instead of detract, but for the most of us it is a thread to be handled with care. For this reason, when a bit of the Western theatre comes our way we eagerly seize it, as shown by the visits of Mischa Elman and Zimbalist and Schumann-Heinke and the rest of their ilk.

There are the threads of the American Legion, and the League of Britons Overseas, and the women's clubs and all the other social and semi-social institutions that strive to be duplicates of those in the countries from which we came. Some of us scoff at them, believing them inferior to the threads which they duplicate, and they may be, but failure to use them makes the pattern less beautiful and our lives more dull.

There is the thread of the Christian Church, a thread which many Japanese are weaving into their own pattern. Except for those to whom the church is warp instead of woof, it is a thread not greatly used in the Far East. The temptations of the Orient are not all active temptations; some are passive.

The thread of literature and reading is highly prized out here, more highly prized than in the places of its manufacture, but not even then so highly prized as its true worth. It is partly the law of supply and demand that gives the printed word its importance. Far from the centers of book and magazine production, we eagerly grasp all that comes our way, and we weave all such into a more prominent place than we do at home. The thread of literature and of the press has come to be one of the threads which stretch around the world and which are woven into the great pattern of the world life of today.

The thread of friendship, too, is more nearly appreciated when far from old friends. New friends are made here, but we do not and can not forget those left behind. Thoughts of them enter more into our lives and, often, have a greater influence in shaping our lives than would their actual presence. Their influence may be as great as the influence of loved ones dead.

We seek eagerly for the threads with which we are familiar to do our weaving. We prefer to use the tried and known. We would rather wear leather shoes than high wooden geta, even when the streets are muddy and the rains pour down. Better, we think, to let our feet get wet than to adopt so strange a custom at which others of our kind would laugh. We seek the threads we know, but the Far East thrusts into our hands its threads, too, and we are forced to carry them over and under the warp, to weave them into the garment which is to clothe us as long as life. A day, a month, a year—long years, in the Orient must color and shape to some extent the brocade of our life.

The noises of the street, the whistle of the hot noodle man, the conch of the seller of fish, the call of the blind masseur at night, the clack of thousands of wooden geta on concrete platform or their steady crunch on loose gravel are permanently woven into the life of him who hears them night after night, day after day. The "Hai! Hai!" of the 'rikisha man and even the "Dochira?" of the tram conductor have become permanent with us. They are mingled with other threads which we can not forget, and so, even if we wish—we can not lose them.

The bounds, the smells, the sights: All are threads which we perforce must use in our weaving. In the loom of each Tokyo Westerner there must be a thread of strong-smelling daikon, a thread of freshly caught fish, a thread of the odour that rises from canals and stagnant pools. These are threads of Japanese origin which we are forced to use, but there are also Japanese threads for which we delightedly grasp, realizing that they will give to the garment of life a richness and a strange beauty that otherwise it would lack.

The gaily dressed children swarming in the temple yard when the matsuri is on, the silks and porcelains and lacquerware, the ghosts and temple bells and clouds of cherry blossoms or of wisteria are threads which we welcome and which we handle delicately as we carry them over and under the warp of life and death and birth, of food and clothing and shelter. They give a gleam of richness and the lustre of silk. They are the little things that count quite as much as do the smells; that count more. We try so to weave that the gaily colored thread of children's laughter covers and hides the thread of muddy, dirty streets. It is because of them that we are contented. We fret and worry and complain, but we are contented.

The big things are here just as truly as in the West, the great broad strands of the warp that stretch along the loom of life. The difference lies in the woof. the shading of the silk or cotton or linen threads which we weave back and forth across the warp. Some threads are thrust upon us; many we choose.

As we choose, so does the pattern of our life appear—a garment of sheer beauty and sunshine that is a joy to wear, or the gray-uncolored cloth of a coat that we slip on to protect us from dreary rain.

THE END

For Product Safety Concerns and Information please contact our EU representative GPSR@taylorandfrancis.com
Taylor & Francis Verlag GmbH, Kaufingerstraße 24, 80331 München, Germany

www.ingramcontent.com/pod-product-compliance
Lightning Source LLC
Chambersburg PA
CBHW051627230426
43669CB00013B/2211